THE
GUN
ARSENAL

THE FIRST GUNNERS

ARSENAL
FROM PLUMSTEAD
TO HIGHBURY

BRIAN BELTON

Pennant Books

First published in paperback 2008
by Pennant Books

Text copyright © 2008 Brian Belton

The moral right of the author has been asserted.

British Library Cataloguing-in-Publication Data:
A catalogue record for this book is available on request from
The British Library

ISBN 978-1-906015-27-5

Design & Typeset by Envy Design Ltd

Printed in the UK by CPI William Clowes Ltd, Beccles, NR34 7TL

Pictures reproduced with kind permission of Hulton Archive/Getty Images.

Every reasonable effort has been made to acknowledge the ownership of
copyright material included in this book. Any errors that have inadvertently
occurred will be corrected in subsequent editions provided notification is sent
to the publisher.

Pennant Books
A division of Pennant Publishing Ltd
PO Box 5675
London W1A 3FB

www.pennantbooks.com

CONTENTS

PREFACE
ARSENAL BELONGS TO ME!

This book gives detail and context to the origins of Arsenal Football Club as a works team of the Woolwich Arsenal. This is something, as an Arsenal supporter, that I have always known, but never allowed to really break through into my consciousness. For me, supporting a football team is all about identity and place, and knowing that the Arsenal's roots were in South London creates a degree of discomfort and rootlessness in me. This is no bad thing as it sharpens my understanding of the role that my part of North London has played in opening its arms to a whole host of 'incomers', as in fact my own family were.

My support has always been closely associated with my childhood experiences of exploring my manor and discovering others who on Saturday afternoons would push and shove their way, shuffling as one, towards Highbury stadium: I was carried with my feet barely touching the pavement as fellow Gooners made their weekly pilgrimage to the ground.

It is difficult to believe that the club's beginnings which seem so firmly part of Islington can have been so far away. What is it that made this club move from South to North London? How could supporters from Woolwich have retained the sense of belonging that I think is so necessary to support a football team?

Although its roots may be elsewhere, there is no doubt in my mind that the Arsenal is still mine.

Rosy Belton (née Adriaenssens
– The Highbury Ragamuffin)

FAN'S
FOREWORD
BY DARREN MULLEY

As a lifelong fan of Arsenal FC, I am delighted to have been given the opportunity to introduce this fascinating book. Brian does a remarkable job in transporting us back to our club's earliest times, charting our evolution from our days as an amateur South London club. Whether we are aware of it or not, history has continually shaped the fortunes of the Gunners, creating the club that we as fans so admire and love. Today, our most visible and clearest connections with this past are the traditional signs and symbols such as our name, shirt and badge. These help construct our identity as Arsenal fans and therefore represent a permanent and powerful display and expression of both the underlying historical foundations of our club and the ongoing significance to us as supporters to this present day. History endures through tradition; this book captures and illustrates the richness of our past and the beginnings that have shaped our club's great traditions.

When I was first asked to write this foreword, I immediately began to reflect on what I already knew of our club's past and, if I'm honest, other than a few fragments that I have picked up on the way, I didn't know that much. This was quite a strange feeling because I have always loved reading about history but I have never taken the time to find out about my own club! But perhaps this is not surprising, given the nature and amount of coverage that football now commands. Our everyday lives are pleasurably saturated with the games, news, gossip, opinions and analysis. We can now access, read and watch dedicated 24-hour TV sports news, online club and fan sites and update texts to our mobile phone about our club; we are so embedded in and devoted to the present, riding wave upon wave of information, we maybe don't have time to put this on hold and step back into time. And, in my view, our move to the Emirates has only reinforced this further. We are not just a club that is fixed in the present or the past any more; we have moved on from our Highbury heritage to become a club that is constantly planning and looking forward in order to successfully compete within the small, domestic 'Top Four' and the other best clubs in Europe, striving to achieve the right conditions for the club to consistently dominate across all competitions.

But this same drive and determination to grow and surpass the present can also be found throughout the early years of our club's history. Brian writes with an obvious passion for the history of football and successfully brings alive the pioneering characters of our club, the games, events and forces in both football and the wider society that laid the foundation for Arsenal to grow and flourish to what it is now. The earliest chapters of our club's evolution are packed with wonderful stories that decorate and enrich this book, demonstrating how the Gunners' great heritage is based on humble beginnings. Furthermore, reading about this is made all the more fascinating when you contrast this history to our club's current status and position in English football. What is therefore so appealing to me is Brian's ability to construct a bridge to cross over and travel back into time to rediscover our club's rich and elaborate heritage – it's so incredibly different from our present-day experiences it is almost like reading fantasy fiction! But our story also connects with my own past too; taking me back to my summer days of organising and playing friendly footie games over the park with my brother and our mates, and to the absence of pitch markings and crossbars, leading to arguments about whether or not a shot should be counted as a goal. For the early pioneers of our great club, I sense that it didn't matter to them either – like us, all they wanted to do was have a kickabout.

Perhaps being able to consider the past is really to be authentically in the present. What seems sure is that, without an awareness and appreciation of our own personal history, we wouldn't have the sense of belonging, purpose and meaning that ultimately defines, shapes and guides us. And so, if we are to truly value our club, I think that we are obliged to explore its history; to build upon and appreciate our existing identities as supporters. In a way, we should feel compelled to seek out this odyssey into our club's past and visit its rich, historical landscape because it reminds us that we all belong to something much larger and greater than ourselves. So, I congratulate

Brian on writing a remarkable book that carves out an intriguing path that enables us to take a tour of Arsenal's fascinating heritage. For me, it has been an enormously satisfying feeling to be reminded that, whether as nations, communities, families or as supporters of football clubs, we are always stronger for making the effort to go on such a journey and to remember our history.

INTRODUCTION

THE FIRST
GAME

In 1886, Blackburn Rovers won the 15th FA Cup Final against West Bromwich Albion 2–0 at the Racecourse Ground (the County Cricket Ground, Derby) after a crowd of 15,000 witnessed a 0–0 draw (after extra-time) at the Kennington Oval. England international inside-left Jimmy Brown scored Rovers' first goal and Joe Sowerbutts claimed the second. This was the first time the FA Cup had been won outside the boundaries of London and it was the third consecutive win for Rovers. It would be two years before Preston North End became the first Football League Champions (Rovers would finish fourth in that inaugural season, with WBA trailing them by two places). And 1886 was also the year the team that would become Arsenal Football Club played their first match; their opposition was Eastern Wanderers, a club that, like so many others, have long since disappeared into the mists of history.

The game took place on 11 December 1886, at which point the footballing entity that would become known as the Gunners had no name, no pitch and no kit. It is likely that the side had to call themselves something, which was probably Dial Square, the name of a workshop within the great Woolwich Arsenal where many of the team members were employed.

That initial encounter was fought out some way from the Woolwich Arsenal and even Woolwich itself. In fact, the team had to cross the River Thames to make their sporting debut. No doubt they used the Woolwich 'free' ferry, as the foot tunnels at Greenwich and Woolwich were not opened until decades later; the old steam ferry ran from the wharf next to the Wapping dock stairs (Tunnel Wharf, previously Middleton Wharf) to Rotherhithe Church. At the end of their 'voyage', the ancestors of today's Emirates 'Galactios' arrived at what passed for a pitch on wasteland, situated where Tiller Road in Wapping now stands, on the Isle of Dogs. Somewhat pleasingly, a sports and leisure centre complex has been built on or near to where the game would have been played.

Elijah Watkins (whom David Danskin, the founding father of the team, had persuaded to become the club's first secretary) described the venue: 'It eclipsed any pitch I ever heard of or saw; I could not venture to say what shape it was, but it was bounded by back-yards for two-thirds of the area and the other portion was ... I was going to say a ditch, but an open sewer would be more appropriate ... when the ball was not in the back gardens, it was in the ditch; and that was full of the loveliest material that could possibly be ... the mud had to be cleaned out of our dressing-room afterwards!'

The team for the game with Eastern Wanderers were: Beardsley, Danskin (captain), Porteous, Gregory, Bee, Wolfe, Smith, Moy, Whitehead, Morris, Duggan.

The result of the game was a matter of argument. With no crossbars (although, this year, the Football Association introduced a 'cross tape' between goalposts as a rudimentary forerunner to them), practically no pitch markings and the ball spending much of the time in the sewer or the backyards, it must have been near impossible to keep track of details. So often was the ball 'dunked', Watkins went on to report, that at one point the players had to scrape off the 'mud'. The local sanitary inspector (Mr Fowler) had previously judged the pitch 'an obvious health hazard' so one can only imagine the sort of residue heading the ball would have left.

But it seems Dial Square, who had strode out for their debut looking magnificent in a diversity of multi-coloured knickerbockers, took the day 6–0.

While this may seem a somewhat ungainly starting point for a great club, the fact that the team had managed to play an organised match at all was the result of the determined, even rebellious, leadership of the club. This game was a testament to men who had overcome much to found their team and was the start of a long and, at times, hard road that gave rise to a football club who have consistently led the way in world football, by way of what have always been the game's most powerful League and Cup competitions, for over close to a hundred years. The consistency, class and contribution of Arsenal Football Club to sporting and social history are second to none and no history of the game is complete without a sizable reference to the mighty Gunners.

The story that follows details how it all started and

how the seeds planted by the lads of Dial Square grew into one of the greatest ever football teams.

Up to 1904, Woolwich Arsenal, the only London-based League club at the time, had been a fairly well-supported Football League side, but, after the club's first promotion to Division One for the 1904/05 season, what were, for the time, phenomenal crowds turned up at the Manor Ground, and throughout the Football League only Newcastle United could better the Reds' (as Arsenal were then nicknamed) average 19,980 home gate.

However, by 1910, Chelsea and Spurs were also pulling in the punters, almost three times as many as Woolwich Arsenal, and even Fulham, although still a Second Division side, were attracting greater numbers than the boys from Plumstead, who were facing bankruptcy.

The 1912/13 campaign ended in an unparalleled disaster for Arsenal: just a single victory at home all season, two on the road, which in turn meant the average gate at the Manor Ground finished well below 10,000. Woolwich Arsenal suffered their first relegation and fell back to the Second Division, with a then massive debt of £3,000.

At this point, a very unusual saviour stepped in.

Henry Norris, the man who would take the team to Highbury and, in 1919, Division One, arrived at the club.

Since the 1930s, Arsenal Football Club have been ranked among the most distinguished in the sport and the Gunners' achievements over recent decades have made this great football institution a globally recognised brand name. But, perhaps even more than is the case for many of their peers, the first years of the club remain something of a mystery for many fans.

In this book, I have sought to piece together the story of the initial and crucial decades of the club, from a time and place very different from where the Gunners find themselves today. From the works team known as Dial Square to the new dawn of Highbury 27 years later, *The First Gunners* charts the foundation of a football phenomenon.

This is a dynamic and absorbing saga. The past achievements of the great red and white giant and all they look certain to accomplish in future years can scarcely match what was undertaken and remarkably realised by the people that forged Arsenal into being; this was perhaps the club's greatest achievement.

However, this book is not just a simple history of the first modest incarnation of the gargantuan football institution that exists today. It is an exploration of part of the embryonic game in London and was motivated by some personal connections with the first years of the sport. I have not tried to replicate the masterful work of Roper (2004) that supplies an exhaustive history of the London and national football and social environment of the late 19th century. The focus of *The First Gunners* is almost entirely on the early development of Arsenal Football Club but this is a tale that squeezes the entire social history of football in London into one compact account. Royal Arsenal started life as a team of working men, scraping together what little they could spare from their hard-earned wages to create a football team. They played on their newly won Saturday afternoons off and every available public holiday. It never occurred to these men that their pursuit would be anything but amateur in nature. However, a few years later, effectively faced with the threat of extinction as other teams began to appear around them in London, the club became Woolwich Arsenal and, in defiance of the authority of the Football Association, turned professional. As outcasts of the game in London and the South East, soon after, the club was obliged to become a limited liability company and as such a fully fledged capitalist endeavour, despite the huge reservations of co-founder and player John Humble. But the side was still effectively staffed, organised and run by working people.

However, following episodes of crowd disturbance and hooliganism (one of which resulted in ground closure for over a month), along with financial difficulties and mediocre on-field performances, Arsenal were brought under the sway of the entrepreneurial power of Henry Norris, a shrewd and fiercely ambitious self-made man. The aspirations and instincts for financial exploitation of this man, wrought in the furnaces of profit-motivated enterprise, transplanted the club from their Kentish/ South London border roots to a proud new stadium, one of the best in the country, set in a quiet district of North London.

By 1913, Highbury represented the 'brave new world' of the game and the version of 'business football' that would explode after the Great War to begin to produce the colossal, swirling black hole that football economics has become. The linguistics of economic chicanery were soon part and parcel of the club's life; allegations of bungs and fraud led to inquiry and banishment in the 1920s. In short, football had become the game we see today.

As such, *The First Gunners* shows us where we have come from, and it is to be hoped that, by having some knowledge of the way Arsenal were born, we will be better able to carry the treasure that has been passed on to us, and with due respect to those that wrought it out of poverty, and the struggle for some time away from hard, dangerous work, to search for joy running in a green field and the simple pleasure of kicking a ball with a few mates.

CHAPTER 1
RED DAWN

While much of the late 19th century was eventful in terms of football, 1886 was able to boast a particularly full calendar. This was a time when the game was still young. The FA Cup was just 15 years old and the Football Association was only eight years its senior. A football pitch consisted of a centre line with no other markings; goals didn't have a crossbar or nets. There was no such thing as a penalty kick and the goalkeeper was able to put his hands on the ball anywhere on the field of play. The referee didn't make any judgements about free-kicks or goals before players lodged an appeal with them and there was no requirement for members of the same team to wear similar colours.

Professionalism in football also 'kicked in' during 1886 (although it had been legalised by the FA in 1885) and, not wishing to be tainted with the stain of filthy lucre, the Scottish FA (founded just 13 years earlier) disallowed its affiliated clubs and players from being involved with English professional sides. This was bound to cause problems sooner rather than later, and, when Blackburn Rovers half-back James Forrest, a professional, turned out for England in Glasgow, inevitably objections were made. The England selectors' slightly macabre solution to the situation was to identify Forrest's pariah status among his amateur compatriots by obliging him to wear a different shirt.

But, more importantly for our story, in 1886, towards the end of the year, close to the border of London and Kent, a small group of mostly Scotsmen were beginning to have the first thoughts that would lead to the birth of a new football team, and at a meeting held at the Prince of Wales public house at Plumstead in October 1886 the club that would be known as Arsenal were conceived.

David Danskin was probably the most vociferous among this sterling company of soccer stalwarts. Born on 9 January 1863, in Burntisland, Fife, as an

18-year-old David was working as an 'Apprentice Engine Fitter at Works' and in 1885 he left Kirkcaldy and came South to take up a post at the Woolwich Arsenal as a mechanical engineer. As a teenager, he had played as an amateur for Kirkcaldy Wanderers, a side that could boast two other future Reds, Jack McBean and Peter Connolly. He could (and maybe should) have followed most of the young men of the area into the Ravenscraig shipyard. But Davie chose to head South, and came to Kent at a time when Europe was locked in a massive arms race that was to be one of several catalysts for the events that would explode in 1914.

Danskin and his fellow footballing enthusiasts were among the many thousands of migratory Scots that flooded into Southern England at this time, as industry, invigorated by the arms race, cried out for labour. Until the end of the 19th century, Woolwich was a completely separate town, only connected to London by geographical proximity. It was mentioned in the Domesday Book in 1086 and the first known reference to the famous ferry, which had been for hundreds of years the lowest public crossing point across the River Thames, was in 1308, when the rights to operate it were purchased for £10. The military

connections began with the building of the Royal
Dockyard and grew when the Arsenal, the Royal
Military Academy, the Royal Artillery Regiment and
the various military hospitals in the district were
built. At the time of the foundation of Royal Arsenal
Football Club, there were 28 military units based in
the area. So Arsenal FC can be thought of as the
progeny of the single most important military town
in England, where, at the end of the 19th century, the
lives of the civilian population would have been
dominated by the physical and social presence of the
massive armaments factory.

The political situation had made arms production
a major factor in the economic life of Britain at that
time and Woolwich was one of the centres of the
'war industry' (and the biggest complex of its kind in
Europe). The huge and thriving government-run
Woolwich Arsenal was of course a kernel of this
trade and, as the manufacture of ordnance was
highly labour intensive during that era, it was a
place of employment for great numbers of people,
many of whom, similar to Danskin, were effectively
refugees from the talons of poverty. The Royal
Arsenal was an enormous employer; its size and
influence was measured on a national scale, drawing

its workforce from the entire country. There was plenty of overtime and the shared love of football among the men that filled its workshops provided them with something of home.

It was Danskin who would be pivotal in establishing a works football team at a time when the county of Kent was resolutely an area dominated by rugby and cricket, although, of course, both these games would have been foreign to a lowland Scot like Danskin. Prior to the mid-1880s, south of the Thames, only Blackheath and Blackheath School could claim any kind of a mention in football history. In 1883, both had sent representatives to the first meeting of the Football Association; however, this noble pair had swiftly transferred their allegiance to rugby, although Blackheath remain the only founder members of the FA to survive as a sporting entity.

Local cricket aficionados, like their rugby-playing counterparts, were not supportive of Danskin or his 'type'. In early 1886, a certain Joseph Smith had attempted to convince Woolwich Arsenal cricket club to allow part of their pitch to be used for football. The idea was given short shrift, although it is unlikely that anyone involved would have been surprised by this reaction. In much the same spirit,

Danskin was informed, in no uncertain terms, that rugby and cricket were the only true sports for Kentish men and that football certainly had no place in the 'Garden of England'.

In fact, Woolwich Arsenal as an institution seemed rather out of place. As one of the country's major munitions factories, it existed in a somewhat inappropriate setting. North Kent was hardly the natural habitat for those choosing or being obliged to work in what was a decidedly dangerous industry. Some said they were a 'rough old lot', peppered with 'rum characters' and 'scallywags' of various creeds and origins. This included both men and women, many of whom worked in the nearby TNT section and were to became world famous. Their skin and hair became dyed a sickly yellow by the corrosive chemicals they used and this provided them with the nickname that would be understood internationally, the 'Woolwich Canaries'. A historical echo of this feature can be found in Arsenal's second strip.

The early incarnation of Arsenal Football Club might have been lost if a couple of former Nottingham Forest players had not turned up looking for work at one of the Royal Arsenal's workshops. Morris Bates and Fred Beardsley would help to ignite the latent desires that would give rise to one of the greatest football clubs in the world of sport.

At that early point, Forest were among the best clubs in England. They were the first Northern club to make the last four of the FA Cup 1879, a feat they repeated in 1880 and 1885 when they took the powerful Queen's Park to two matches with Beardsley in goal.

The old Forest ground at Trent Bridge had an ordnance factory (Chilwell) as a neighbour, where Beardsley (and probably Bates as well) had worked prior to taking similar work at Woolwich. They seemed to inspire Danskin, together with his friends John Humble, Elijah Watkins and Richard Pearce (a Bolton man), who recruited 15 of their fellow workers to each contribute 6d (2$\frac{1}{2}$p) to set up a football club.

John Wilkinson 'Jack' Humble had joined the 'Radicals', a group of left-wing political activists, very soon after moving from County Durham to look for work and settling in Kent. The Radical Club building still exists on Walmer Terrace, opposite Plumstead Station, close to where the main entrance of Woolwich Arsenal's Manor Ground once stood. It was later to become an entertainment venue.

Humble, who would go on to join the nascent Socialist Party, was a fervent believer in workers' rights from his earliest years. Naturally, he supported the movement for shorter working hours and more time for leisure activities, which included his passion, football. Along with Danskin, he felt that all working men should have the opportunity to take part in Association football. Danskin backed up his sentiments with a donation of a further three shillings (15p) of his own money (he would have been earning between 30s and 35s a week at that time, probably for at least 50 hours' work). The first thing the club bought was a football. This would have been a bespoke item in those days, probably handmade to specifications, and, as such, it would have made quite a hole in the club's restricted funds. Initially the ball was used at lunchtimes, the only part of the day the lads had free to practise their skills.

It wasn't Fred Beardsley's first experience of starting a football team within Woolwich Arsenal. During 1884, he had assisted in forming another side. Many years on, he told his grandson, RA Beardsley-Colmer, that the first club had been named Woolwich Union, and had staged their games in Plumstead, at a venue known as 'Piggy' Walton's field, part of what was known as Plumstead Common (the closest public space to the ordnance factory). Beardsley took his passion for football wherever he went. In 1887, he started a new job with Siemens Engineering (which is now of course a global concern) but he was fired for taking too much time off work to play the game. Fred would eventually become a director of Woolwich Arsenal.

It is likely that at least some of the men who turned out for Woolwich Union were part of the new club, but it would be wrong to suggest that Union were the precursor to the Arsenal, principally because Danskin and John Humble were seemingly not implicated in the organisation of the earlier club. It is probable that both before and after 1886 there were other football teams made up of workers from Woolwich Arsenal and it is likely that the best performers who turned out for Royal Arsenal played for a number of them. However, it is generally agreed that the club Danskin organised, Dial Square, are the direct ancestor of today's club, as the testimony of John Humble confirms. Humble, who was to be connected with Arsenal for a longer time than anyone else in his era, became the club's informal historian (with Danskin making a smaller contribution), and his records indicate an unbroken chain of events between

1886 and the team that would give rise to Arsenal Football Club.

Dial Square, basically a double courtyard, was the gun machining complex. One courtyard housed turning shops and smithies while the other was made up of armourer's shops and accommodation. It was just one small facet of the sprawling Arsenal site, situated in an area known as the 'Great Pile'.

A few tens of metres from Dial Square, from 1787, stood the Royal Artillery cadets' quarters. The young officers in training would use the lawns that existed between Dial Square and their place of residence for drills and sport. Today the whole area has been integrated into a housing, entertainment and historical estate, which includes a museum devoted to the Arsenal works and the Royal Artillery Museum 'Firepower'.

Danskin and Humble understandably allied their own experience, the tale of their involvement from the earliest time, with formally organised football in Woolwich Arsenal. But it is possible that, if another player, for example Beardsley, had taken on the role of honorary secretary, then a different story about the origins of the club might have been written.

It is hard to speculate about the motivation of the 15 men who joined up with Danskin, Humble, Watkins and Pearce from this distance in time. They may have joined for fun, exercise and/or social reasons. Certainly at the time there was a vociferous movement against what was then known as 'spectatorism' that wanted to see more men actually playing games rather than watching them. The case was put most strongly a few years later in a report in April 1891 by the London Playing Fields' Committee, an influential group consisting mostly of ex-public schoolboys committed to extending facilities for playing football and cricket in the Metropolitan area: 'The English love of sport, perverted by want of opportunity for active exercise, produces the gambler and the loafer. Men who, under better conditions, might have developed into active and healthy English people, degenerate into mere spectators at athletic contests, which might almost be compared to gladiatorial shows held by professional giants for the idle amusement of a puny crowd.'

Canon Barnett was the founder of Toynbee Hall, the university settlement in Whitechapel. Its youth workers encouraged football in the many clubs set up by the settlement in East London in the late 1800s.

Barnett saw the positive aspects of games as forms of rational recreation, but objected to a man 'exciting himself over a match or race where he does not even understand the skill'.

His wife, who apparently agreed with him on most issues, disapproved of 'the football matches, which thousands watch, often ignorant of the science of the game, but captivated by the hope of winning a bet or by the spectacle of brutal conflict'.

From the 1870s onwards, people had the opportunity to see the top players of the day in action in their local parks and playing fields. With no more than a chalk-mark around the perimeter of the pitch, even many major FA Cup matches could be viewed free of charge. This probably motivated great numbers of boys to take up the game and almost certainly the spectacle and entertainment these matches offered would have cultivated a taste for watching the sport among the large numbers of youths and adults attracted to these contests.

However, 'old boy' clubs, made up of former public-schoolboys, had an ambiguous attitude towards spectators. In line with university settlement and the public-school mission attitudes, they saw the potential for football to contribute to improving working-class life and to the character development of young men, but believed this lay in playing the game rather than merely watching it. For all this, there were contradictions. The crowds that came to cheer these 'gentlemen' sides on in their notable FA Cup campaigns were not turned away and, when admission costs were charged, the noble amateurs did not decline to accept their share of the proceeds of the gate money paid by the large crowds who had come to watch the matches.

From the late 1880s, fixtures involving the top London amateur teams drew gates of more than 2,000. Contests with professional clubs could attract more than 4,000 spectators. Clapton introduced season tickets in 1890 at the cost of four shillings. This gave admission to the club's 24 home matches and was accompanied by promotional information about friendlies against professional clubs like Nottingham Forest, West Bromwich Albion and Notts County.

It is clear then that a culture of paying to watch good-quality football had been firmly established by the end of the 19th century. From the modern perspective, it is hard for us to appreciate that, in football, spectators preceded fans and supporters. In the late 1800s, football was essentially an athletic event; in its working-class incarnation it was close in spirit to the Powder Hall sprint competitions in Scotland and the local athletic events familiar to Northern working-class towns and villages. If you were working class you went to a cock fight, a boxing match, a cycling, running, horse or dog race, a dog fight or a football match to take in a spectacle, which was enhanced by the opportunity to speculate on the outcome of any competition by way of a wager.

As such, it is likely that the first players recruited from the Woolwich Arsenal were well attuned to spectatorism and its potential. With this came the ancestor of the original working-class motivation to watch sport that is still with us; but the culture of spectatorism was fuelled by gambling. If it was just success that was needed to attract supporters, most games would not have been well attended for much of the time. The wish/desire to 'support the side', to create a sense of loyalty to a name and ideals associated with that name, had not yet been transplanted from the culture of public school or university. However, interestingly, today that ethic is fully developed in the form of fan loyalty. What we see today as 'supportership', something steeped in working-class mythology, actually has its roots in the ambitions that a ruling elite had for those they wished to control. This group wanted working men to play and watch the game purely for these reasons, but these values were totally foreign to the men from pits, factories and munitions works who took up playing and/or watching football; they gave little thought to the future, of what their team might become.

There were thousands of groups of young men dotted around the country similar to those first 15 at the Woolwich Arsenal but whose identical efforts would never reach a history such as this. Naturally, only a tiny number of these sides were to rise, by good fortune, trickery and some genuine endeavour, to national prominence over the next century. But we can be sure that at least some of Danskin's men came together with the hope of pulling in some interested spectators and perhaps even making some money by their own enterprise and wagers; they gave up time and made a significant commitment to their team, after working long, dangerous and taxing shifts.

Evidence of the most likely date for the start of Danskin's new club comes via the record of those first subscriptions that were made in October 1886, although it is impossible to name a particular day on which the founding of the Arsenal Football Club took place. Apart from those already cited, men named Whitehead, Price, Porteous, Ratcliffe, Brown and Gellatly were also recorded as having paid their subscriptions (two others failed to be recorded). Danskin, Humble, Beardsley and Brown all survived to see Arsenal win the FA Cup for the first time in 1930.

CHAPTER 2

ROYAL ARSENAL

After their first match, the victorious team from the Woolwich Arsenal workshops assembled in the Royal Oak public house, next to Woolwich Arsenal Station, on Christmas Day (that fell on a Saturday in 1886) with a shared eagerness to take things forward and address the immediate needs of their football club, most importantly to agree on a name, acquire some kit and find somewhere regular to play their games.

The first option for a name was Dial Square, as it was the common factor for most of the team. One of many workshops that were part of the Royal Arsenal at Woolwich, it had been designed by Sir

John Vanbrugh and Nicholas Hawksmoor, whose other distinguished projects included the design of Blenheim Palace, which was built for the Duke of Marlborough.

Dial Square was built between 1717 and 1720, but got its name after a large sundial had been placed above the entrance to the square in 1764. The facade of the building can still be seen, including the sundial. The structure is located between Woolwich and Plumstead, which partly clarifies why the team from the workshop never actually contested a game in Woolwich.

But the idea of calling the new football club Dial Square was quickly passed over in favour of Royal Arsenal (although their adopted name may have led to insinuations by some that the Woolwich side had delusions of grandeur, taking such a regal-sounding name without even having a permanent ground). For some time, it was thought this choice might have been the consequence of combining the name of the pub where the players' meeting was convened with the men's place of employment, but the players' shared workplace was often referred to as the Royal Arsenal. Although there were other sides emanating from different workshops within the ordnance factory, it seems plausible that the team that were to be called Royal Arsenal would be an amalgam of all, or at least some, of these sides. In any case, the name would allow for recruitment from the whole of the workforce's available footballing talent, although Danskin and his men must have felt they could hold the title well enough. Whatever the circumstances, the name was to endure up to 1891, when Woolwich Arsenal was formally adopted. However, the Football League continued to refer to the club as Royal Arsenal until 1896 (possibly because of the suggestion of royal patronage).

Red was the chosen colour for the club's shirts for the simple reason that Bates and Beardsley had red shirts from their time with Nottingham Forest. Until 1909, first-class keepers like Beardsley wore the same shirts as the rest of the team. Players usually provided their own shorts, or 'knickerbockers' as they were called in those days. In the early 1800s, football boots were not specifically designed for the game, but were mostly sturdy, standard, shop-bought footwear that the players themselves adapted by nailing iron bars across the soles. But eventually, in 1863, all projections from boots were banned, and the first specialist boot appeared in 1886. In 1891, the FA allowed the use of studs and bars, although they had to be made out of leather.

As the Royal Arsenal could not find the money for their shirts, Beardsley contacted his former club with a request for assistance. In 1865, Forest were the first club in England to wear red when they started donning caps of that hue. The kindly Forest administration dispatched the necessary shirts to their former custodian and also included a ball in the parcel, which was helpful (to say the least) as the Royals had lost their own ball. When they next took the field, the new club looked like a replica of the Nottingham Forest side, at least in terms of their initial appearance. Since that time, with the exception of the 1895/96 season, Arsenal have always worn red and white. (The characteristic white sleeves were added by legendary manager Herbert Chapman, who, looking to distinguish his side, introduced them prior to a game at Highbury vs. Liverpool on 4 March 1933.)

With a name and kit secured, the next task for Royal Arsenal was to find a field on which to play. Their choices were limited due to a lack of funds, so they needed any expedient public land within practicable travelling distance; so Plumstead

Common, a local green area about a mile from the Arsenal open to everyone, it was. However, it was not the level, agreeable recreation ground perhaps suggested by the title 'Common, but a bumpy, undulating area, peppered with sharp stones. It was also furrowed by the Royal Horse Artillery who used it as a training ground, which left it littered with holes, ruts and deep wheel marks and covered in horse dung.

A section of the old Common can still be found, but housing development has taken up most of the once open area. It is impossible to find out where Royal Arsenal might have placed their goalposts in preparation for matches (there is no record of exactly where their pitch was; indeed, it is possible that they played in different spots on the Common each week) but between games they were stored in Fred Beardsley's garden, which backed on to Plumstead Common.

These are humble origins, but other current Premiership clubs had similar beginnings. Tottenham Marshes were home to Spurs (known in football circles at the time as the 'Marsh-dwellers') for a period of five years before the club chose to fence off an enclosure, in part to protect themselves from rowdy spectators who were in the habit of slinging clods of mud at their team when not happy with their efforts, and also to create a much-needed form of demarcation to allow them to charge an admission fee. However, perhaps the strongest motivation for the embryonic Tottenham team to create a more secure space was the repeated purloining of their diligently marked-out pitch by other sides.

The Reds (as Royal Arsenal were almost immediately nicknamed) asked Erith, another local team, to meet them on Plumstead Common on 8 January 1887. This was the first game the team played as Royal Arsenal. That first Arsenal side was: Fred Beardsley, David Danskin and Porteous at full-back, Gregory, Price and Wells at half-back, while the forward line was Smith, Moy, Whitehead, Creighton and Bee.

The home side won 6–1.

A further eight games were played before the season ended on 26 March, and overall Royal Arsenal lost just two of their first 10 matches – 4–0 away to Millwall Rovers (whose progeny would be Millwall Athletic and today's Millwall, but who immediately became the Reds' most ardent local adversaries) and 1–0 visiting the 2nd Rifle Brigade. Millwall were beaten 3–0 in the penultimate game of the term at

Plumstead. The Royals (the team's other nickname at the time) had scored 36 goals and conceded just eight. It was a promising start.

CHAPTER 3

A CHANGE OF MANOR

1887/88

Although the team had used Plumstead Common during the 1886/87 season, it was clear that this could not continue to be viable as a home ground. Even when the Royals had tried to play respectable football, the cleft-ridden surface effectively stifled any effort to refine their game. The team moved on to the Sportsman Ground in Plumstead for their second season. This was an old pig farm, part of the property of local pig-breeder Mr Walton, which was roughly the same location where Woolwich Union had played, situated on the edge of Plumstead Marshes.

The Royals entered the London Senior Cup for the

first time. Around 500 people turned up in October 1887 for the first-round meeting with Grove House on the Sportsman Ground. Some accounts indicate Grove House had conceded this tie prior to the match date, as they had been unable to field a full side and that the game was played as a friendly. But a match was certainly played and a 3–1 win, with goals from Potter, J Creighton (his brother, R Creighton, also played in that game, and they were the first brothers to appear together for Arsenal) and Morris, together with the facility of another home draw, made it look as if the Woolwich men were in for something of a run. However, a sound 4–0 beating by Barnes ended their hopes.

The basis of the side was Beardsley and Joe Bates, although the team also boasted some skilful and experienced Scottish players (in fact, at one time Scotsmen filled eight of the available places on the team sheet). Bates (who was to die at the tragically early age of 41 from tuberculosis) was known as the 'iron-headed man' because of his regular use of his forehead, an uncommon trait during a period when match balls, wrought out of thick, heavy leather and laced with chunky strands of harsh rigging, were almost deadly (especially when caked in drying mud and/or ice). Both the former Forest men had been subjected to punishing physical workouts while at Trent Bridge, which put a particular emphasis on developing leg muscles, and perhaps it was their influence that caused the *Kentish Mercury* to note that the Royals had 'thighs like oak trees'. Indeed, Royal Arsenal became known as one of the most aggressive and toughest collections of players. Even before a ball was kicked, stories about the lads from 'the sinister factory' who laboured behind 20ft-high walls were rife among the opposition. The men of the Arsenal seemed mysterious, as they were not even allowed to talk about the nature of their work beyond the confines of their workshops.

As winter began to turn to spring, the wet weather worsened the propensity of the Royals' pitch to become waterlogged, even after the most moderate of showers. On the morning of 30 March 1888, Royal Arsenal were looking forward to their home game against local rivals Millwall Rovers, but when the club committee arrived they found the playing surface submerged. It was Good Friday and a large crowd had been expected at the now-unplayable match. The neighbouring field (that was mostly used for pastureland) just up Manor Road, in the direction of Plumstead Station, seemed in good condition. Following frenzied activity by club members, a pitch, including fixed goalposts, was laid out. The match ended in a 3–3 draw, and for the next two years (1888–90) the Manor Field (which would be renamed the Manor Ground) would be the home of Royal Arsenal. Some records place the move to the Manor Ground as 11 February 1888 (another encounter with Millwall), and it is probable that games were played there from that date onwards, but it seems the Good Friday situation settled the matter as a more permanent arrangement. The site was next door to what is known as Royal Arsenal East, facing Plumstead Station, and some of the workshops of Royal Arsenal East formed a backdrop to the Manor Ground. Today, apart from the name of the main road (Manor Way), nothing remains to suggest that at one time 25,000 people watched football on this site, where Manor Way, a roundabout and the Plumstead Bus Garage now stand.

The Manor Ground pitch was cordoned off for match days using wagons, loaned from the nearby barracks and the Arsenal munitions factory itself, with ropes attached between them to create a designated playing area (to keep supporters off the pitch). The wagons also served as makeshift stands if a big crowd was expected ('big' was anything up to 1,000 people).

In all, Royal Arsenal played 22 friendly matches during the 1887/88 season. Twelve wins were recorded, four draws and four losses (the outcome of the other two games have been lost in time), and the Reds scored 36 goals and let in just eight. The first game with Tottenham, on the Spurs ground on Tottenham Marshes on 19 November 1887, ended in a 2–1 defeat for Arsenal. The Reds had arrived late and the game was abandoned because of poor light with a quarter-of-an-hour left to play – this was not unusual in the days before floodlights. The only known report of this match appeared in the *Weekly Herald* on Friday, 25 November. It told how Spurs 'at once began to attack, but 10 minutes from the start Arsenal scored a lucky goal. From this point the visitors were pressed throughout, and had it not been for the splendid defence of F. Beardsley (Notts Forest) in goal, the score would have been much larger. Through darkness the game was stopped.'

But the Royals defeated Spurs 6–2 when the North Londoners crossed the river in February.

The Manor Ground quickly acquired a reputation

all of its own, thanks largely to the massive engineering works close by and the proximity of the Southern Outfall Sewer, the major liquid waste disposal for all South London (this is argued by some to be the root of the chant 'Arsenal shit'), and the massive pipe still exists today. Sporadic seepage of untreated effluent often brought a new meaning to the phrase 'stinking up the pitch'. This, together with the monstrous sight of the great industrial fortress, spewing out its toxic amalgam of chemicals and filth, discharging putrid, odious gas over the Woolwich home turf, must have made visiting players feel they had landed in Hades.

That season, the Reds fielded their inaugural junior XI (what would later be called a reserve side), who played three games, winning one and losing two.

Royal Arsenal adopted their first crest in 1888, which featured three cannon viewed from above, directed northwards, similar to the coat of arms of the Metropolitan Borough of Woolwich. Looking at the crest now, it is easy to mistake the cannon for chimneys (especially considering the club's connection with the factory where they originated, although Dial Square had no structures of that type), but the carved lion's head and cascabel (the knob at the end of a cannon, cast on to the gun barrel, to which ropes were attached) on each confirm that they are cannon. This crest would be abandoned following the move to Highbury in 1913, but, in 1922, the club instituted their first single-cannon crest, eastward-pointing, with the inscription 'The Gunners' alongside it (in 1925, the cannon was reversed to point westward and its barrel was slimmed down). So it was in the early 1920s that Arsenal's modern nickname became established, although it had been in supporters' and media vocabulary for some time because of the club's original association with the ordnance factory. Although the Reds as a nickname stayed in common parlance until after the club relocated to North London (as their original support base melted away), by the late 1930s the Arsenal were universally known as the Gunners.

CHAPTER 4

'CHAMPIONS OF THE SOUTH'

1888/89

From their first stirrings, Royal Arsenal developed an informal scouting network that operated through the connections that existed between munitions factories across the country. Promising players were recommended and could be found work in the Woolwich Arsenal. Rivals may have grumbled about Danskin's and Humble's enrolments, but, at the time, many works teams functioned in much the same way.

The Royals' initial seasons saw them achieve success on a local basis. Throughout November to early December 1888, the team got the better of Phoenix, Dulwich and Old St Paul's, scoring 10 times while letting in only three goals, to reach the last four of the London Association Cup.

The Reds line-up for the semi-final on 19 January was: Beardsley, J Creighton, McBean, Brown, Bates, Danskin, Morris, R Creighton, Connolly, Charteris, Scott.

But it was Clapton that went on to win in the Final after defeating the Royals 2–0 at their Spotted Dog Ground in Leyton. It was in that match that David Danskin sustained the injury that curtailed his playing career, after which he rarely kicked a ball in competition again.

From November to February, the Reds plied their trade in the Kent County Challenge Cup. A 6–2 victory over Horton Kirby and a 5–1 trouncing of Iona was followed by a six-goal draw at Gravesend, the Arsenal goals coming by way of Bates, Charteris and Connolly. But the Royals were disqualified for refusing to play extra-time, as they believed that they had actually scored more goals than their opponents.

Twenty-four friendlies were played in 1888/89. Only eight were recorded as being played away from Plumstead, and Arsenal notched up 10 victories, nine losses and five draws (two matches could not be traced). The best performance of these matches was the 1-0 defeat of Tottenham at Northumberland Park (the North Londoners had by this time escaped the exposed marshes).

Despite these promising beginnings, Royal Arsenal were still living hand to mouth, and players would often be involved in collecting entrance money.

THE FIRST SILVERWARE

On 12 October 1889, the Royals defeated the 5th Northumberland Fusiliers 6-1 in Plumstead in the Kent Senior Cup. This was the start of a tremendous series of victories in that competition; the Reds beat West Kent 10-1 and Gravesend 7-2 to take them into a semi-final meeting with Chatham on the Chats' home turf. A hat-trick from Jim Meggs and contributions from Robertson and Offer pushed Arsenal to a 5-0 victory and into their first Cup Final. The Reds' defeat of Thanet Wanderers 3-0 at Chatham resulted in the first silverware won by an Arsenal team. Barbour hit a brace and Offer was again on target.

The Royal Arsenal side that day were: Beardsley, Connolly, McBean (the full-backs both hailed from Kirkcaldy), Howat, Bates, Julian, Christmas, Meggs, Barbour, Robertson, Offer.

The 'Kent double' was achieved when Royal Arsenal's juniors (the reserves) won the Kent Junior Cup.

The Royals were also involved in the London Senior Cup, and the ties were being played during roughly the same period as the Kent Senior Cup games; for the most part, the Reds fielded the same team that had won the Kent Senior Cup (although Arthur Christmas stood in for Richard Horsington in the London Senior Cup Final).

The Royals got to the Final of the London Senior Cup (the leading competition for London clubs at that time), scoring 17 goals in the four matches that took them to Kennington Oval, then home of the FA Cup Final, to meet Old Westminsters, a team founded in 1885 and made up of old boys of Westminster College, who were based at The Limes Ground, Barnes, London. To that point, the Reds had only conceded three goals in the competition. But at the Oval, in front of 10,000 spectators (by far the biggest crowd the Arsenal players had entertained), the Reds were narrowly defeated by the only goal of the game, and Old Westminsters retained the trophy they had won in 1887.

But, just a month later, the Reds evened the score when they beat Old Westminsters to claim the prestigious London Charity Cup in front of another crowd of 10,000, this time at the Spotted Dog Ground, Leyton. The team that won 3–1 were: Beardsley, Connolly, McBean, Howat, Bates (captain), Julian, Christmas, Offer, Barbour, Robertson and Fry (sometimes known as JC Edwards).

Arsenal made their debut in the FA Cup in the 1889/90 season, playing in the qualifying rounds. The 'English Cup' was the most important and demanding football competition in the world at that time, although the first three ties didn't really stretch the Reds. Lyndhurst were completely overwhelmed 11–0. Thorpe (later to evolve into Norwich City) couldn't find the money to pay for a trip to London from Norwich for the replay after a 2–2 draw in East Anglia, which meant Royal Arsenal went through to meet Crusaders. As in the previous round, the game was drawn at 2–2 after 90 minutes, but three goals in extra-time sent Royal Arsenal into the last of the qualifying rounds. However, on 7 December, at Plumstead, a 5–1 defeat by Swifts (a side that included several international players who were inspired by the famed EG Bambridge) ended the Reds' Cup run. That game provided the biggest ever crowd at the Manor Ground, when around 6,000 turned up, despite an earlier snowstorm.

It always took some time for the ground to empty on such occasions, as there were only two exits leading on to a private road, which required the London County Council's permission to be used. This often meant that fans who had taken a drink before, during and/or after the match would relieve themselves at any convenient place as the crowd dispersed. As this could create a near flood at times, more experienced match-goers would manoeuvre themselves conveniently closer to the exits as the game came to an end.

In Arsenal's Cup exploits, Barbour, with 17 goals, was the club's top scorer, followed by Robertson (13), Meggs (11) and Scott (7). A total of 24 goals were also shared between 13 other players.

In 1889, Royal Arsenal felt justified in calling themselves 'Champions of the South' through their successes in the various Cup competitions. They hit 81 goals in their 24 friendly games (of which all but six were home matches), conceding just 30 as they claimed victory 17 times, and experienced only three defeats (just one at Plumstead). The Reds certainly looked an entertaining and winning side and the growth in attendance began to reflect this; newspaper reports at the time noted that more than

1,500 attended a game with Spurs in September 1889. This was to be the performance of the season: the Reds won 10–1!

On 31 May, Royal Arsenal entered and won a six-a-side contest organised by the National Physical Recreation Society at the Agricultural Hall, Islington (about a mile from Highbury). The Reds beat London Caledonians 15–7.

When Arsenal first moved to the Manor Ground, the players normally used the Green Man in Plumstead High Street, the Railway Tavern (which was conveniently close to the Manor Ground, beside Plumstead Station) or The Star on Common Road (which still exists, in a refurbished state) to change, wash and be 'refreshed'. But increased crowds began to make it difficult for players to get to the pitch from these local hostelries. In response, a disused railway hut began to be used as a rough and ready changing-room. It was another sign of the increasing popularity of the club and of the game itself.

CHAPTER 5
INVICTA

1890/91

The 1890/91 campaign saw Royal Arsenal shine in the London Senior Cup. In the first round, Old Westminsters (now old enemies) were defeated 4–1 at the Spotted Dog Ground, Leyton. But a protest by the Toffs from Barnes led to a replay being ordered. Attempts to get the game played at the Oval on 20 December and at Leyton on 10 January failed due to poor weather conditions, and the tie was eventually replayed on the last day of January at the Oval. Following a 3–3 draw at full-time, extra-time ended in a 5–4 defeat for the Arsenal men. Another protest followed, this time by the Reds, claiming the

Westminsters had fielded an ineligible player. Yet another replay was called for, but in a fit of pique Old Westminsters scratched from the competition.

A 3–2 win over Casuals in the quarter-finals followed. The semi-final against Clapton was fought out at the Kennington Oval, and the Reds came back from 2–0 down to hit three goals in the last 25 minutes of the match. This set up a meeting with St Bartholomew's Hospital in the Final at the Oval, and the Royals won their first London Senior Cup, thumping their opponents 6–0 with goals from Barbour (2), Offer, Fry, Connolly and Gloak. The Arsenal side were: Edward Bee, Peter Connolly, John McBean, David Howat, William Stewart, John William Julian, Arthur Christmas, Henry Offer, Davis Hubert Gloak, Fry.

This was Royal Arsenal's biggest success to date; the *Kentish Independent* told the story of the response: 'Excitement is a mild description for the scenes in Woolwich and Plumstead on the return of the football champions on Saturday night. A host of admirers met them at the Dockyard Station and drove them in open carriages, shouting and singing. There were celebrations everywhere all evening and, we fear, a good deal of drinking was mixed with the rejoicing and exultation.'

However, the London Senior Cup was to be the only silverware of the season. In the London Charity Cup, after a second replay of a second-round tie, the Reds were eliminated at Leyton (2–1) by Old Carthusians (Old Boys of the Charterhouse public school, Godalming, Surrey, who had won the FA Cup in 1881).

The competitions in which the Royals made their mark over the first part of the 1890s were demanding contests. Although the London FA during this period enforced a stern amateur ethos, Royal Arsenal had the benefit of being a works team. Quality players were provided with employment at the Woolwich Arsenal by the supportive management, who gained kudos and good public relations from their high-performing football team. Occasionally, the club would even buy out the contracts of football-playing soldiers who they spotted stationed at the barracks near by or who were enlisted with the Horse Artillery. This seems to indicate that Royal Arsenal had solid financial backing from the parent company.

The Royals' reputation as a hard side continued and the teams that had faced players of the ilk of Morris Bates, John Julian and Jimmy Charteris in Plumstead were often a battered crew after games, limping home both relieved and bruised, telling stories of butchery in the environs of Kent. Two days before Derby County's FA Cup first-round game against the Reds in 1891, the *Derby Post* on 15 January reported confirmation of the situation: 'One of the Derby chaps was heard to mutter that: "A journey to the molten interior of the earth's core would be rather more pleasant and comfortable an experience than our forthcoming visit to the Royal Arsenal."'

Of course, at times the Ordnance men could expect to get as good as they gave, although John Julian, a Woolwich midfielder, took it on himself to retaliate against retaliators. He was invariably being treated for ankle or knee injuries, and believed that most of the damage he sustained had occurred in the process of him fouling others. Julian had started work at the Arsenal in 1889 and became the club's first professional captain two years later. (A feature of the era was that players often appeared as guests for other clubs and later in his career Julian is recorded as turning out for Luton.)

Another Arsenal 'deterrent' was Jim Charteris, who had the task of regularly berating the referee, looking to ensure that decisions went in his team's favour (something we often take as part of the modern game but, in fact, seems to always have existed). Charteris came from what today might be called a 'difficult background'. Born out of wedlock (a terrible slur at that time), as a kid, Jimmy had witnessed his bigamist father taken to jail, and he had been placed with a series of family and friends. Joining Arsenal caused the Scot to be snubbed by his own community. In October 1887, the *Motherwell Times* declared, 'He will find out that he has made a sad mistake. There is little honour playing for some of these English clubs.'

Jim sadly died in poverty from a suspected heart attack aged just 28.

At the Manor Ground, while people were getting a free, if not entirely hazard-proof, view from the increasingly infamous sewage pipe, paying customers were becoming cramped as the Royals' games were averaging crowds of around 5,000 per fixture. Following the successful Cup runs of 1889 and 1890, the Reds had decided to relocate to a new ground across Plumstead High Street during September 1890. Following investigations, the Invicta Recreation Grounds, a few hundred yards from the Manor Ground, appeared to be the best option locally and the Reds would make it their home between 1890 and 1893, leasing it from George Weaver, of the Weaver

Mineral Water Company. The Invicta (the Latin word translates as 'undefeated' and, as the motto of the county of Kent, has a heritage going back to the Norman Conquest) was seen by many as the finest ground in the South. On the south side, it had a grandstand that could accommodate around 1,500 people, and, on part of the west side, there were concrete terraces able to hold about 3,000 (traces of that terracing can still be found in some of the gardens in Hector Street, SE18). The playing area was 130 yards by 90 yards. The site had dressing rooms and these and the other facilities promised to make life easier for everyone concerned with the club. It was a multi-purpose facility and had been used principally as a cycle track, which formed the ground's perimeter. Sunday cycle meetings often attracted five-figure crowds and a lot of 'informal' gambling. The Invicta had the advantages of being close to Plumstead Railway Station and of having an entrance for carriages in Butcher's Lane.

Arsenal had been excused from the qualifying rounds of the FA Cup but, in front of a then record crowd of 8,000, they were knocked out by Derby County, who beat them 2–1 at the ordnance men's new home ground.

The Reds were involved in 27 friendlies during the first full season of the 1890s, and played only five times away from Plumstead. With a goal account of 72 for and 41 against, they won 17 times and lost just five games. In Cup competitions, Barbour was the highest-scoring player with seven goals, followed by Offer with five. Perhaps their most interesting encounter of the season took place on Easter Monday 1891. The club, looking to capitalise on their growing popularity, organised an Easter Tournament, culminating in a game against that year's Scottish Cup winners Heart of Midlothian, which attracted 15,000 paying customers.

Attendances of 8,000 had become regular, and it cost 3d (1p) for entry, which included entertainment from the 2nd Kent Artillery Volunteers, who supplied a selection of music (a tradition carried on at Highbury many years later). The band became a major attraction and often the crowd would sing along to well-known tunes; 'Oh Promise Me' (by Reg DeKoven and Clem Scot) was an early favourite but after 1900 few ditties could match the enduring popularity of Harry von Tilzer's 'A Bird in a Gilded Cage'. The band often reappeared at the conclusion of games to send fans home to musical accompaniment, a process which could take over an hour as many stayed to listen and sing to the music (somewhat defeating the object). Unaccompanied half-time and pre-match communal songs included some immortal verses that were often sung in the hop-fields of Kent, 'I Painted Her' and 'I-Dingle-Dangle' (an ode to a prize cow) being among the most often heard.

Although they were doing well, against professional teams, as well as the leading amateur sides, Royal Arsenal were lacking something (as the 5–1 thrashing by Hearts demonstrated – although Hearts also held the FA Cup holders Blackburn Rovers to a draw that year). The Reds had beaten the likes of Cambridge University, Old Harrovians and 1st Highland Light Infantry 5–1, but they lost by a similar scoreline to Everton and were beaten 3–1 on their own turf by Sunderland (the Football League Champions in 1891 and 1892; in fact, in the four seasons from 1892 to 1895, the Black Cats would be Champions three times and would finish as runners-up in 1894).

After the FA Cup game with Derby, two players, Peter Connolly and Bobby Buist, who performed well in that match, were approached by County's skipper, John Goodall (who was also the club's acting secretary-manager), who offered them professional contracts. Ultimately, Buist and Connolly failed to join Derby, but the Reds had lost a number of their most promising players to professional clubs. Goodall's move on the players, together with the perceived need for the club to 'kick on', as they seemed to have reached a ceiling in terms of on-field results, caused Royal Arsenal's committee to initiate the chain of events which would change the history of the game, taking the club into the Football League and playing a big part in the campaign to establish the Southern League.

CHAPTER 6
HUMBLE PROFESSIONALISM

1891/92

During 1891, John 'Jack' Humble, a Royal Arsenal committee member and occasional goalkeeper, who, like Danskin, did not suffer fools gladly, became frustrated by how easily his team's best players could be enticed to join Football League clubs. The Woolwich Reds still saw themselves as the 'Champions of the South' and they certainly appeared to have overtaken the likes of Millwall and Tottenham Hotspur, who had been formed before them. The Royals were still ostensibly an amateur club (although their players were almost certainly provided with 'expenses'), but there was nothing preventing them joining the ranks of the professional clubs. Humble understood that for his club to advance a courageous move had to be made. He was not wrong. Hundreds of clubs, many of which Royal Arsenal had played during their brief history, would disappear over the coming years, because they were either unable or unwilling to reinvent themselves in tune with events and time.

The vast majority of the clubs based south of Birmingham collapsed in this bull-market environment, in which finance and location played big roles. Teams in a county like Kent, being not terribly well off and hard to reach, were at a distinct disadvantage. But the recent Factory Acts had provided the likes of Danskin and his men with Saturday afternoons free from work, and the 19th-century Reform Acts had extended the franchise, in itself bringing a taste for democratic activity into the lives of many working people. This was a time before the maturing of the Labour Party and when trade unions were organisations still in the bud; workers who argued for improved housing, health care, working conditions, wages or leisure activities were often seen as subversive.

It is arguable that Humble is second only to

Yorkshireman Herbert Chapman and his chairman Henry Norris, in terms of influence on the history of Arsenal Football Club. Born in the village of East Hartburn in County Durham in 1862, Humble, who arrived in Woolwich about the same time as Danskin, was typical of the men who founded the club and worked at the Arsenal. After his parents died within three months of each other, in 1880, Jack, along with his elder brother Arthur, determined to leave the comparatively depressed North East to look for work. However, not having the money for train fares and being known for their obduracy, they walked the approximately 400 miles to London from Durham, a feat which made the headlines back in East Hartburn. They obviously both found work quickly, as, by the time of the 1881 Census, they were recorded as engine fitters at the Arsenal.

The story of the Humble brothers was not unusual for the hard times. The Arsenal employed relatively large numbers of poor men from the North of England, the Midlands and Scotland, the likes of Danskin, Beardsley and Humble, many of whom brought with them a type of ball skill that was yet to be established in the South, most notably the art of dribbling.

Royal Arsenal's Annual General Meeting in the summer of 1891 was convened at the Windsor Castle Music Hall. Jack Humble proposed that the club take the gamble of turning professional in the hope of ensuring that better players would not continue to be tempted away to teams that were able to reward them financially and free them from laborious work. At that stage, it had been rare for more talented individuals to stay with the Royals for longer than a year. Jack's idea was carried by a big majority. It is likely that the change of the club's name to Woolwich Arsenal was connected with turning professional. It was seen as almost an act of sedition in some quarters for professional sport to have a direct or suggested aristocratic patronage.

Objecting to an additional proposal that a limited liability company be formed at the same time, Humble told the meeting, 'The club [has been] carried by working men and it is my ambition to see it carried on by them.'

A letter to the *Kentish Independent* queried the notion of integrating football with commerce: 'The funding of a soccer club should be left to the working men and those who know the game. Surely allowing clerks or accountants to control a football club through buying shares is a retrograde step.'

The proposed move appears to have been seen as undesirable in 1891; seemingly, it was taken to be against the sporting spirit that the club wanted to foster and (correctly as it turned out) a threat to the power-base of the working men who had formed the club.

At that stage, it seemed football was increasingly becoming a battlefield in the class war. The Association game had been the traditional preserve of public schools, but it was slowly transforming into a working-class endeavour. As the 20th century dawned, football in the South remained the stronghold of upper-class rule over the sport, while the North made it a more proletarian pastime. But literally thousands of amateur works teams were frenetically jockeying for position, urgently working to draw the best of local talent. Some had ambitions to replicate Northern sides, and turn professional.

The London FA unreservedly rejected any form of what it saw as the Northern malaise of professionalism, a sentiment that had hardly been questioned by the capital's clubs. This was to be a thorny issue for another 15 years that concluded in an almost complete schism in 1907 after the London, Surrey and Middlesex FAs founded the Amateur

Football Association as a completely separate body from the official FA.

But in the summer of 1891 the London FA instantly barred Woolwich Arsenal, their former Cup winners, from any competitions under their patronage and expelled the club from their Association. Although predictable, these actions posed a real threat to the existence of Woolwich Arsenal.

At an extraordinary general meeting of the London FA, held in Anderson's Hotel, Fleet Street, the chairman of the meeting, Mr A Jackson, fervently denied having formerly called professional footballers 'wretches', but later he was to confess that he 'despised the little tricks of the game' that those outside the amateur ranks practised. Jackson told the *Kentish Mercury*, 'I wish to pay a high compliment to the press generally for the stand they have taken against Woolwich Arsenal Football Club.'

The chairman of Old Harrovians, Mr John Farmer (who had been a music teacher at the Harrow School, whose old boys supplied personnel for the team, and co-wrote many of the famous Harrow School songs with his colleague Edward Ernest Bowen), reminded the meeting that the majority of amateur clubs allowed players 'extremely liberal travel expenses' and that Woolwich Arsenal were, to their credit, 'up front about it all'.

The vote to expel the Reds was relatively close, 76–67, but it meant that the team were disbarred from Kent and London football and restricted to playing friendlies against other professional clubs from the North or the Midlands, and FA Cup games.

Woolwich Arsenal's first professional game was staged at the Invicta on 5 September 1891. There is no record of attendance, but it was likely to have been a full house that watched Sheffield United win 2–0.

Royal Arsenal contested 57 friendly games in the 1891/92 season, all but half-a-dozen of which were home games. They lost only 16 times and were held to draws on just eight occasions; they hit 181 goals and let in 102.

David Danskin put himself up for election to the club's committee in 1892, but he failed in his attempt, which ended his official association with the club. He later played a part in organising a new works team from the district, Royal Ordnance Factories, but they disappeared around 1896. Davie would often act as referee in local games and he continued to attend Arsenal home matches; his son, Billy, was also involved, having sold programmes at the Manor Ground as a boy.

In that first professional season, astute promotion drew in locals who took the opportunity to view the great Northern and Midland sides including West Bromwich Albion, Sheffield Wednesday, Glasgow Rangers and Preston North End.

Although financially crucial, progression in the FA Cup was never likely, especially as the Reds were excused the qualifying rounds. Woolwich Arsenal's debut in the competition in January 1892 was a first-round away tie at Small Heath (the club that would become Birmingham City), where the Reds were well and truly beaten 5–1 at Muntz Street.

CHAPTER 7

FORWARD TO THE LEAGUE, BACK TO THE MANOR

1892/93

Woolwich Arsenal's 1892/93 season was a case of more of the same, with the Reds achieving some success against what were really better teams, the likes of Sheffield United, Sunderland (the League Champions that term), West Bromwich Albion, Aston Villa and Third Lanark (one of the powerful Scottish teams of the era). The side were back in the qualifying rounds of the FA Cup. They saw off the Highland Light Infantry 3–0 at the Invicta, which set up what was to be a 10–1 Plumstead victory over City Ramblers (Jim Henderson, Charlie Booth and Arthur Elliott all scored hat-tricks, George Davie got one). A third successive home tie followed and Millwall Athletic (the Dog Islanders having recently dropped the 'Rovers' appendage in favour of 'Athletic') were effectively defeated by an own goal by the Lions' keeper Obed Caygill in the five-goal game.

In the fourth qualifying round, Arsenal were drawn to play at Clapton but the Tons elected to meet the Reds at the Invicta and paid the price in a 3–0 defeat. This put Arsenal into the first round proper, and a Newcastle Road meeting with the mighty Sunderland. Three months earlier, the Wearsiders had thrashed the Reds 4–0 at the Invicta. The Black Cats had won the Football League Championship the previous season and would achieve the rare accomplishment of retaining the title (they had only been elected into the Football League for the 1889/90 season). The following term, Sunderland would finish runners-up only to be Champions again at the conclusion of the 1894/95 campaign. As such, the Mackems were one of the most powerful sides around at that time. This being the case, few were surprised outside of South London when the tie ended in a 6–0 defeat for Woolwich Arsenal, witnessed by 4,500 Plumstead fans.

This was not the best news for the club from a

financial perspective either. The Reds had to find some means of generating income and a good idea was badly needed as the team were haemorrhaging the life blood of their support. The best solution seemed to be to form a Southern version of the Football League that could provide a solid and reliable competitive schedule. Woolwich Arsenal convened a meeting of likely potential members of the new League on 24 February 1892 in Fleet Street at Anderson's Hotel (the same location at which the Football League itself had been founded four years earlier). Although the informal suggestion of calling the proposed contest the Southern League was not well supported, alternatives like the First/Second Division South were not popular either. Initially, there was a definite enthusiasm to make something of the idea, perhaps with the winners being able to negotiate a place in the Second or even First Division 'proper'. Twelve sides were elected: Chatham, Chiswick Park, Crouch End, Ilford, Luton, Marlow, Millwall, Old St Mark's, Reading, Swindon, West Herts (the side that would evolve into Watford) and Arsenal. Tottenham (with whom relations were already tense as Spurs believed that they were competing with Arsenal for support) finished last in the poll, and as such were not elected;

they had gained just a single vote (probably their own). Nine years on, Spurs were to be the first Southern professional club to win a top honour when they won the FA Cup.

The London FA were unsurprisingly outraged, warning that it would mete out the same punishment to the other 11 clubs as it had inflicted on Arsenal should a 'rebel' League be formed, and all the would-be insurgent clubs cowed under the pressure of the threat. However, the plan was resuscitated the following year by Millwall and this time there was enough courage (and necessity) to see the idea through.

Arsenal's joint top goalscorers in their friendlies, with 30 apiece, were Jimmy Henderson and Arthur Elliot (who played in all 52 games that season to be the most consistently present performer). Gavin Crawford, a Scot who appeared 31 times during the term, was the first professional imported by the club in 1891. It was indeed an odd season, which included a 6–6 draw with Cambridge University and an 11–0 win over Sevenoaks.

TO THE LEAGUE

However, Woolwich Arsenal, without any real local competition, were in a desperate situation. There appeared to be just one chance left: application for membership of the Football League. There were good teams in the district, the likes of Millwall Athletic, Dulwich and Clapton, but with the FA ban hitting them hard it would become increasingly difficult for Arsenal to compete with better sides. The amateur game would continue to exert itself in South London for many years, pulling in support and boasting a host of good players. Arsenal's distinctive place in the capital's football milieu had been undermined at a surprisingly swift pace and their hand had been forced.

The odds were stacked against the Reds, the club having never played in a League competition, but, at the conclusion of the 1892/93 term, the Football League decided it would expand the Second Division (in its second season), adding three clubs to the existing dozen. Arsenal's chances for election to the League were even more favourable when Bootle failed to be re-elected to Division Two and Accrington (one of the original 12 founder members of the Football League and not directly related to the famous Stanley) declined the opportunity to take up a Second Division place following their relegation from Division One. This meant that there were then five vacancies for entry into the Football League. Rotherham Town and Newcastle United were given membership without a vote being taken; Liverpool, Woolwich Arsenal and Middlesbrough Ironopolis were elected at a subsequent meeting. (Ironopolis were a professional splinter team from Middlesbrough Football Club that were formed in 1889 but would be dissolved in 1894 when they lost their Paradise Ground home.) There were just two other candidates recorded: Loughborough Town and Doncaster Rovers (the latter would have to wait until 1901 for election).

Liverpool (who won 18 votes), Newcastle (4) and Arsenal (13) between them would become England's top club an amazing 35 times up to 2007.

Perhaps it was providential that Woolwich Arsenal applied for entry to the Football League at a point when there were so many vacancies. Normally, they would have stood little chance, and even at a stage where two new vacancies presented themselves (the most that might usually be expected) the Reds' chances of getting voted in would have been minimal. Fate? Destiny? Lucky Arsenal?

The Woolwich side's decision to throw their lot in with the Football League was something of a gamble. Firstly there would be immediate additional costs. If the Reds struggled, there was no plan B; the team were so reviled in the South they had effectively burned their boats. But they had nowhere else to go.

George Weaver, Arsenal's landlord at the Invicta, was quick to respond to the potential of the club's election to the League. In expectation of the increased income that would be generated by the big crowds who would come to watch teams like Birmingham City, Notts County and Manchester City, with less than three months before the new campaign got under way, Weaver informed the club that he was raising the ground rent; he offered them a new one-year lease costing £400 with an additional £100 to cover rates and taxes. Following negotiations, the lease component was reduced to £350 per year on condition that Weaver would be elected on to Arsenal's club committee.

During Arsenal's 1892/93 season of friendlies at the Invicta, the club had paid £200, including rates and taxes, for an eight-month lease, which in itself was very over-priced as most Football League clubs were not paying even half that much at the time. Wolverhampton Wanderers paid £76 a year for their lease, and Sunderland just £45, and the average for a Football League club was certainly less than £100 a year. However, since moving into the Invicta, Arsenal had also spent £60 a year on repair bills.

Weaver probably believed the club had no choice, but, after he turned down a reported final offer of £300 inclusive for the year, the committee felt unable to meet this huge added expense and as such were once more obliged to move.

Ultimately, Arsenal's departure from the Invicta was the end of the stadium and eventually Weaver built two rows of houses on the site, Hector Street and Mineral Street.

At that stage, so close to the start of the 1893/94 Football League season, with no ground, only moderate support and no obvious playing resources, the difficulties must have appeared insurmountable. However, the club had continued to use the Manor Ground for training and practice and as such it was familiar to the players and supporters. Following long discussions, it was agreed that the club should purchase that ground or acquire a short lease and continue to look out for an alternative to buy so that the club might be able to control their own destiny and be free of unscrupulous landlords.

Following negotiations, Woolwich Arsenal brokered a deal with the Manor Ground's owner, and purchased the plot (opposite Plumstead Station). To acquire the 13.5-acre site for their new ground, Woolwich Arsenal paid a reported £4,000. Just over five acres were developed for the football ground.

However, it was not enough just to buy the Manor Ground: extensive improvements were necessary. The club were not going to be able to house supporters with wagons and ropes, as they had done during their first period of occupation at the Manor, particularly after having become used to superior facilities at the Invicta.

The list of work seemed daunting, but, with the financial and physical help of their supporters, the club laboured through the summer of 1893 to prepare the ground for the Second Division. Those few months saw a massive effort, mostly by volunteers, to ensure the Manor Ground would be fit to house League football.

The playing area needed levelling to remove a considerable gradient, which was achieved by using a foundation of hardcore, and this also helped to drain the marshy plot. Wagons full of loam and earth were deposited on the site and spread to make a level surface on to which the finest available turf was laid.

The pitch was roped off and low-level fencing was erected around the boundary of the playing area when the rest of the work was concluded.

Supporters were accommodated by the erection of a five-tiered terrace on the north side of the ground along the length of the pitch (over time this was extended all around the ground with the original terracing being covered by an iron stand that was able to enclose around 2,000 people). Fencing, mostly of galvanised iron, was added to encircle the area. Iron was also used to create buildings on the south side of the ground, including changing rooms for the home and away sides, as well as a committee room for meetings. A modest press box for a dozen reporters was also erected, but this was never to house as many as 12 hacks at any one time.

In spite of earlier objections, there was no other way to raise sufficient finance than to form a limited liability company. So, in the summer of 1893, the new company (Woolwich Arsenal Football & Athletic Company Limited) had a nominal capital of 4,000 shares at £1 each. Accounts on the take-up of shares differ, but newspaper reports of the time indicate that around 2,500 were issued to approximately 1,500 people (the remaining shares were left unissued). This left the club a long way short of their target, but season tickets at 10s 6d (52$^{1}/_{2}$p) boosted finances and helped to meet the cost of the procurement and development of the ground.

The majority of the shareholders lived in close proximity to the Manor Ground and were manual workers at the Arsenal. There were just three holdings of 20 shares or more, the highest being 50, which were held by the owner of a coffee house. The first board included a builder, a surgeon and six engineers from the Arsenal.

Any and every means of raising money was tried at one point or another – an archery competition (which astoundingly produced funds amounting to £1,200), raffles, open days. At one point, with bailiffs threatening, Humble resorted to Woolwich High Street to find a club director. Mr GH Leavey, a well-known outfitter, was evidently persuaded, as it seems he felt convinced enough to give an immediate donation of £60 almost literally from the till. This covered the team's wages for the following week and a long train journey to that weekend's away game.

A reported 12,000 squeezed on to the terraces in November 1893 for the FA Cup third-qualifying-round encounter with Millwall Athletic. Few would have believed this possible just a few months earlier.

The Manor Ground was to be the club's home for the next 20 years. Of course, no one then could have imagined that the club's next move would have taken the team so far away from their early home.

According to two players of the time, John McBean and JW Julian (speaking in 1948), the club grew incredibly swiftly during that era because of the government's armament policies (looking to match and better the perceived threat posed by the French at the time), which brought thousands of men to work in the Arsenal and to serve in army units based in the Woolwich district. This created a supply of players and supporters including migrant Scots and men from Northern England and the Midlands, whose game of choice was not readily available in what was, in a sense, a no-man's-land between South London and Kent. The result was that Plumstead became something of a footballing sanctuary.

Unfortunately, Davie Danskin could not accept the direction the club had taken and turned his back on Woolwich Arsenal during the 1890s. The 1901 Census shows that by that time Davie had left munitions work and had started a business building and selling bicycles at 60 Herbert Road, Plumstead. The Danskin family later moved to Coventry where David was employed in the car industry. Their residence was badly damaged in a German bombing raid in 1940 and sadly all his football jerseys and medals were destroyed. He died in 1948, but he had witnessed the great achievements of Herbert Chapman's Arsenal in the 1930s.

The summer of 1893 was a crucial time for the future of football. After a long battle, the Scottish FA accepted professionalism at their AGM in the same month as Woolwich Arsenal were admitted to the Football League. In January 1894, 16 Southern clubs agreed to establish the Southern League (around half of whom were professional at that time).

These choices were major steps on the path to the Football League being accepted as a legitimate part of the game. They were also instrumental in obliging the FA to generally accept professionalism as a fact of life (although there was a serious challenge to this situation from the champions of amateurism during the First World War). The Plumstead men had played a part in motivating much of this huge seed change, to a level far outweighing their size and history as an institution. It is almost staggering that Woolwich Arsenal, a team that in 1893 had a relatively modest history, had played such a significant role in the transformation of the sport and made a major contribution to its development.

Adversaries might have abhorred the actions of what they perceived as the munitions factory upstarts, but the Reds had made a courageous stand on the issue of professionalism and faced a powerful foe head on. The League may have seen that admitting the belligerent Londoners would have been likely to encourage others to challenge the authority of the FA, which of course would increase the influence of the Football League. Within seven years of their establishment, Woolwich Arsenal were members of the Football League; it had been a swift ascent up the game's hierarchy, one of the fastest of all the early League clubs (Bradford City and Chelsea went directly into the Football League without kicking a ball, but that was in the early 20th century). However, this was more the result of the club's commercial insight than the team's record on the pitch.

But the work was just beginning; the two decades

between Woolwich Arsenal's joining the Football League in 1893 and their departure for Highbury in 1913 were to be demanding years.

CHAPTER 8

PLAYING WITH THE BIG BOYS

1893/94

On 2 September 1893, Woolwich Arsenal played their first game in the Football League, which was against Newcastle United, another newly elected club, at the Manor Ground. However, the match nearly did not take place as the *Daily Journal* reported, 'It has been common gossip of late that money was needed.'

The 'gossip' was mild compared to the actual situation. In fact, just before the game, the Newcastle directors were obliged to attend a crisis meeting and take a collection to raise the cash for the team's third-class tickets to London. The Geordies had no money for even the most basic bed and breakfast hotel. Having caught the Friday evening train, they arrived in London early on Saturday morning, a journey of close to eight hours. The tired Tynesiders, many of whom had never visited London before, staggered around a few of the capital's sights in the hours they had before the kick-off, too fatigued to be thankful that it was a bright, pleasant day. They arrived at Plumstead exhausted. Several of the weary travellers grabbed a little sleep on bales of straw (used to dry or insulate the Manor Ground pitch) and had to be woken up a few minutes before the start of the game.

Skipper Joe Powell won the toss for Arsenal. Woolwich, being at home, seemed to have the advantage in terms of the 'first-night' nerves syndrome. But, although they had little in the way of established support, their ground having had to be built from scratch, and not much money, it seems they had managed to get ready and they hit the ground running. The game began with some swift moves and both sides looked eager to make a respectable start to their respective League careers.

After 10 minutes, stylish passing by Elliott and Booth opened the way for Walter Shaw, Arsenal's centre-forward, to score his side's debut League goal. It had been the result of some skilful play and tardy defending.

The Newcastle men, knowing the world was watching, pressed forward in the closing stages of the first half, sending the Reds on the retreat. Powell, Buist and Howat worked hard to maintain their side's lead, while Williams pulled off two great saves to prevent the fighting Magpies getting back on level terms. The teams went into the break with the Geordies feeling justifiably unlucky not to have equalised.

Woolwich doubled their lead in the third minute of the second half. Booth had made an impressive raid down the flank, crossing for Arthur Elliott to score with an unstoppable drive that went in off the underside of the bar.

From this point on, the Londoners seemed to lose a little focus as the game degenerated into an untidy, fragmented affair. But, when Newcastle began to regain their composure, Arsenal seemed to come back into the match.

With less than 15 minutes of the game to play, Tom Crate halved the difference between the teams, scoring Newcastle's inaugural League goal (although some newspapers reported Willie Graham was the scorer). Five minutes on, with Arsenal looking all over the place, a home defender handled close to his own goal. Birmingham's Mr T Stevenson awarded the free-kick and Jock Sorley got his head to the ball to equalise. (Sorley was probably the most tired player on the pitch. He had not slept at all on the train and had had little sleep most of the Thursday night before the trip to London, kept awake by his baby son's nocturnal teething problems.)

After the fourth goal, Arsenal seemed to buck up and both sides then went all out for the winner, but in the end a draw seemed a fair result. The Reds had thrown away a two-goal lead and it was clear that two seasons of friendlies and no more than a few cursory excursions into the FA Cup had blunted the Londoners' killer instinct; they should have finished off their visitors when they had the chance. But the hosts had shown themselves to be brave and ready to work at making themselves a life in the Football League.

The attendance figures for the match are a matter of some dispute, with available records showing huge discrepancies, and there could have been anywhere between 2,000 and 10,000 at the game. In fact, early football reporting was often full of completely inaccurate information about crowd sizes, goalscorers and scoring times. This was in part due to some reporters developing the habit of pocketing the expenses they were given to attend matches and making up their reports from hearsay or brief, makeshift interviews with supporters hours (sometimes even days) after a game. The propensity for newspaper men to share a few bottles of brandy during matches to hold off the cold of the winter game probably didn't help either.

The home team had looked much like the side that had fought out the previous season: Charlie Williams, Joe Powell (captain), William Walls Jeffrey, Danny Devine, Bob Buist, Dave Howat, Duncan Gemmell, Jim Henderson, Walter Shaw, Arthur Elliott, Charlie Booth.

The Magpies had also fielded a useful side: Andrew Ramsay, Harry Jeffery, John Miller, Robert Crielly, Willie Graham (captain), Joe McKane, J Bowman, Tom Crate, Willie Thompson, Jock Sorley, Joe Wallace.

On the same day, Gillingham-based New Brompton played their first ever match (a friendly) with Woolwich Arsenal's reserve team; Arsenal won 5–1.

The Woolwich men had to wait some time for their initial League victory, which came on 11 September in a home game vs. Walsall Town Swifts, when John Heath claimed a hat-trick in the 4–0 result. Two years earlier (almost exactly, on 14 September 1891), Heath, playing for Wolves against Accrington, had scored from the first penalty ever awarded in an English first-class game.

In the latter part of September, Arsenal made the trip to St James' Park for the inaugural Football League match at the home of Newcastle United, but this landmark in the history of the Magpies was witnessed by a paltry crowd of 2,000. However, Newcastle thumped their visitors, scoring half-a-dozen without a response from the Londoners, who felt the full gravitational force of the infamous Gallowgate slope. Newcastle knocked in four goals in the second half, running at the Reds downhill. Wallace and Thompson finished the game with a hat-trick each in what was something of a surprise for both teams in terms of the magnitude of the victory.

Burton Swifts also hit the Londoners for six in November, but the Reds cracked home half-a-dozen themselves twice during the season, away at Middlesbrough Ironopolis and Northwich Victoria (who dropped out of the Football League that term).

During this season, Woolwich were without a recognised keeper, and William Jeffrey, a full-back, played 12 matches at left-back and 10 protecting the rigging.

In this debut Football League campaign, Arsenal finished ninth out of 15, with 28 points from 28 games. It was a creditable performance. Liverpool, undefeated all season, won the Second Division Championship – that was not to occur again in English football history.

In the Cup, Arsenal went through the first four qualifying rounds very comfortably; Ashford United shipped a dozen goals without reply, Clapton were defeated 6–2, Millwall Athletic were beaten 2–0 and the 2nd Scots Guards, providing the Woolwich men with their first away fixture of the competition that season, went down 2–1 after extra-time. This meant a first-round-proper tie against Sheffield Wednesday at the Manor Ground. Wednesday (they did not actually add 'Sheffield' until 1929) had been to the Cup Final in 1890 and they would win the trophy in 1896, so it was no surprise when they came away from Plumstead with a victory. But Arsenal gave them a game, before going down 2–1.

Woolwich Arsenal had equipped themselves well enough. An honourable League placing and a Cup run that had ended in valiant defeat under their collective belt had shown them to be worthy of their League status.

SECRETARY-MANAGER

The role of a secretary-manager was quite complex, not altogether comparable to that of the manager in the modern game. Many secretary-managers were deskbound, dealing with transfers, publicity and low-level commercial and administrative work. They often delegated the readying of the squad to the trainers, what would be called coaches today, who could usually be distinguished by their cloth caps and roll-neck woolly jumpers. Trainers, who had always been part of the game, were, in the main, ex-players, but, as professionalism spread, the majority of boards had realised that these men were mostly unprepared for managing in the professional environment of the business the game had become. The 'secretary-manager' that evolved out of the sport was usually a man with knowledge and experience of the game, but who could also respond to a board's wishes in terms of finding and developing players.

While some boards continued to have a heavy influence on team selection, most also had other commercial interests to attend to (in Arsenal's case, they had to go to work!) and so needed a person who could undertake the day-to-day duties involved in running a team.

In 1894, Sam W Hollis was appointed secretary-manager, relieving Bill Parr (one of the original Dial Square players) who had taken on many of the responsibilities associated with the role. Born in Nottingham in 1866, Sam had little in the way of football experience, having previously worked for the Probate Office and the Post Office, but, although he wasn't a professional manager as such, he was the first individual to be placed in almost complete charge of Arsenal's team affairs.

CHAPTER 9
SOUTHERN SOFTIES?

Woolwich Arsenal became members of the Football League when the club were the only professional side in London and their nearest opponents were more than 120 miles away, with no League clubs south of Birmingham and Burton. This being the case, admitting the Woolwich side had constituted a bold move by the League, although it also entailed the League breaking into the Southern market and all the potential that represented.

However, because of the distances involved, most journeys to and from Plumstead would need to be overnight commitments, and this would have considerable cost implications for every club in

Division Two. Added to this, Woolwich Arsenal were far from their days of drawing big crowds away from Plumstead, and the trip to London would not appeal to many away supporters. The FA Cup was normally the measure by which new applicants to the League were assessed in terms of their playing credentials, but Woolwich Arsenal did not have much form in that competition, having never been able to move beyond the first round proper. It was a hurdle they would not get over for the rest of the 19th century.

But as a body the League Management Committee (LMC) had the prescience to see the benefits of having a London club in their midst; the League could never be seen as a national institution if it failed to include the capital in its number (there would be four more London clubs in the Football League 15 years later – Spurs, Chelsea, Clapton Orient and Fulham).

However, there were some benefits to being thought of as the 'team who played at the end of the earth' as the *Liverpool Tribune* described them. Clubs like Newcastle United and Rotherham hated the long journey South to the London/Kent borderlands, particularly when rail travel was so dawdling and unpredictable. And, even when Arsenal's Northern cousins finally reached the capital, Plumstead was not easy to access from most destinations north of the Thames or east of Greenwich; there was at least a 40-minute, trying journey from Cannon Street Station to Woolwich in a jam-packed, dirty, smelly steam train, which became increasingly stuffed with Reds fans as they neared the ground.

The location of the Arsenal home ground even had a detrimental effect in terms of the team's potential to attract local support. From central London, it was at least half-an-hour further on a tram than the nearest major club (which was then Millwall Athletic), and an awkward place to access by train, even though the Manor Ground was literally just over the road from Plumstead Station (with main access from the Griffin Manorway; the ground had three gates in all). It was remarkable that the team sometimes managed to attract five-figure crowds and suggests the football must have made a difficult trip worthwhile.

The tribulations of the journey were evidenced by one consistent attendee at the Manor Ground. Before the First World War, George Allison was a junior sports reporter with *London Hulton Press* and he was given the regular job of reporting Arsenal matches. He was to generate quite a few tales of his treks from Fleet Street to Plumstead which he found 'heavy going. Other sports writers were more than happy when I offered to undertake all the reporting of Arsenal's home games – meaning I wrote about them for most of the Saturday, Sunday and daily papers, often doing ten different reports [on the same] match. The payment I received softened the monotony of the long and tedious journey [Allison was, as a result, called 'George Arsenal' by his peers]. One could travel on the South Eastern and Chatham Railway from London Bridge, Cannon Street or Charing Cross. The trains stopped at every station. There were the same halts on the return journey, with the added difficulty that no one knew where the trains were going. I once travelled back with a soldier, who asked a porter on Plumstead Station where we were going. "London Bridge," he was told. At the next station he asked another railwayman. "Charing Cross," was the answer this time. He asked again at the next station and was given a third answer. Eventually he told one railway official "You're a bloody liar, you don't know where it's going."'

However, travel was probably less arduous than at any other time in previous history and as time went on Manchester and Liverpool would be under five hours from London by the swiftest locomotives.

Finding accommodation for the night in the district of Woolwich was also fraught with difficulty, as most 'decent' hoteliers were reluctant to fill weekend rooms with a crowd of working-class lads from 'up North'. Often, by the time the opposing players got to Woolwich, they were hungry, tired and irascible – not the best state of mind to play football against a very physical Arsenal side.

Some of the Northern clubs may have thought of Woolwich Arsenal as no more than Kentish yokels, to be taken advantage of a couple of times a season. But soon the Plumstead lads became widely detested, not simply for their rudimentary 'kick-and-run' tactics, but also because of the propensity for uncouth behaviour on the part of both the club's fans and players (on and off the pitch). Woolwich Arsenal understandably attracted an 'interesting' mixture of squaddies and munitions workers to their fan base, a combination that was unlikely to give much of a welcome to opposing supporters or players. A letter of grievance sent to the *Kentish Independent* during the era complained about 'the conduct of fans who spouted foul language and coarse abuse'.

During one game, the referee felt obliged to abandon the match due to the crowd's swearing and, at another encounter with Wolves, a band of soldiers ran on the pitch and thrashed the referee, an ex-Wolves player. The attack, understandably, had the official screaming for assistance (which was worryingly slow in coming). This incident resulted in the Manor Ground being closed for six weeks.

But this wasn't the only such incident. After Arsenal's 1–1 draw with Burton Wanderers in Plumstead, the *Kentish Independent* had reported in January 1895, 'The one topic of conversation this week in football circles and in all circles at Woolwich and Plumstead has been the assault committed upon Mr. Brodie, the official referee in the match on the Manor Field, Plumstead, last Saturday, between the Woolwich Arsenal and the Burton Wanderers Clubs. About 7,000 spectators were present ... Of course the great multitude of people felt profound regret for the outrage, not only for the sake of the principal sufferer and the true spirit of the game, but from well founded apprehensions of consequences.'

Further evidence of the hostile reception to be expected in Plumstead came in the *Newcastle Echo*, who described the scheduled appointment at the Manor Ground as 'an annual visit to hell'.

But much of the 'excitement' on the part of the

club's supporters had gambling at its root rather than any passionate affinity to the football team and was not something particularly related to the nature of factory workers or feckless soldiers. As the *Kentish Independent* wrote of the Reds fans, 'These were not weedy uneducated hooligans but well-dressed middle-aged gentlemen.'

However, at least as significant in terms of the general ill-feeling towards the Reds were the actions and attitude epitomised by Jack Humble and David Danskin. In the last years of the 19th century, this pair had constantly pushed the limits of the Victorian football establishment. They had carried a hard-edged, single-minded professionalism that rammed up against the sort of amateurism that dominated the game in the South of England during that era.

CHAPTER 10

UPS AND DOWNS

1895/96

In their second season in Division Two of the Football League, Woolwich Arsenal bettered their debut campaign, finishing eighth, three points above Manchester City. Following the incident involving the Arsenal players and the referee, which had closed the Manor Ground, the game with Burton Swifts was played at New Brompton (the club that would become Gillingham FC). Arsenal won 3–0. The match with Leicester Fosse (an exciting 3–3 draw) was staged at Leyton. Successive home games on 6 and 12 April 1895 produced a 7–0 win over Crewe and a 6–1 victory over Walsall Town Swifts. But, in the Cup,

Arsenal made their exit in the first round, after losing to Bolton 1–0 in Lancashire.

It was in this year that Arsenal briefly adopted club colours of red and light blue vertically striped shirts, but this livery was not favoured.

Woolwich Arsenal were soon to gain their first representative honours. In April 1895, goalkeeper Harry Storer was selected to play for the Football League vs. the Scottish League. Like many quality players, Harry left the club fairly swiftly, joining Liverpool in December 1895. Six men were tried between the posts in an effort to find a replacement for Storer. John Boyle, who played 10 games in all that season, scoring one goal from half-back, turned out four times in goal.

In 1896, the Reds improved their placing in the League yet again, finishing in seventh, just one point behind Manchester United.

Caesar Llewellyn Jenkyns, skipper of Woolwich Arsenal in 1895/96, became the first player to gain a full international cap while playing for the Reds when on 21 March 1896 he was a member of the Welsh team that faced Scotland at Carolina Port, Dundee. The home side scored twice in each half of the game without reply from their visitors. Jenkyns, a muscular man with a focused attitude, did not stay long at the Manor Ground, but his time there was indeed profitable. It was believed his selection for the side could double the attendance. He had a reputation as a 'serious drinker' during his time with Small Heath (Birmingham) prior to his arrival in Plumstead, although most players in those days seemed to like a drink. Jenkyns had left the club before the start of the 1896/97 campaign.

1896/97

Perhaps the most depressing game of the 1896/97 term was Arsenal's visit to Loughborough Town. The home side pulverised the travelling Reds 8-0 on 12 December 1896.

This was a strange period for Woolwich; between 17 October and Christmas Day 1896, their League results were: a 3-5 defeat at Walsall, a 6-1 win over Gainsborough Trinity, a 7-4 loss to Notts County, a 5-2 defeat by Small Heath, after which there were victories over Grimsby (4-2) and Lincoln (3-2); then came the debacle at Loughborough, followed by a 4-2 win over Blackpool and a 6-2 Christmas Day pounding of Lincoln. In nine matches, Woolwich Arsenal had hit 32 goals and let in 34 – seven goals per game. Despite this extraordinary goal-rush, the club had no outstanding scorer (Peter O'Brian was the Reds' top marksman with just 14 nets). However, it seems watching Woolwich was entertaining even if their results were erratic (to say the least).

The Loughborough result stands as Arsenal's record defeat to this day. In defence of the Reds, their regular goalkeeper Bill Fairclough had been replaced by John Leather, but the keeper's role had been a problem for Woolwich for some time, and Fairclough himself had let in 23 goals during his previous half-dozen outings, so this is perhaps not the most convincing excuse. A much better defence is the fact Arsenal had been compelled to play two games that ignominious day, although they had fielded their reserve side in the FA Cup at home to Leyton, where the Reds won the tie 5–0.

Despite Arsenal's well-deserved reputation for meting out brutality, the only football fatality of 1896 was Woolwich's own Joe Powell, the club's first captain in the League and the team's right-back. He was a powerfully built man who, like a number of players in the Woolwich years, typified the side's rugged and physical style of the day. He died following complications from a broken arm which became infected after an away encounter with Kettering Town on 23 November in the United League. (Arsenal played many other matches in a number of competitions outside the Football League and FA Cup matches, as well as, by today's standards, a huge number of friendlies.)

Arsenal were back in the qualifying rounds of the Cup (entering the fourth round at this stage). After beating Chatham in the fifth qualifying round, a devastating defeat by non-League Millwall (4–2 away) followed. This, together with their first season of non-improvement in the League (10th place), was to signal a seed change for the Arsenal committee.

In April 1897, secretary-manager Hollis joined newly established Bristol City; he was to have three distinctive tenures with the Robins. He left in March 1899 to become secretary-manager of Bedminster, but, when they merged with Bristol City in 1900, Hollis was seen as surplus to requirements. In 1901, he returned to Bristol City and was to lead the Southern League side to runners-up spot and promotion to the Football League.

In March 1905 and up to 1911, Hollis took on the

management of a hotel (he had run a pub between 1899 and 1909). Sam was back at Bristol City for his third spell as manager in January 1911, but City were relegated to the Second Division and he departed Ashton Gate for good in April 1913. But, seemingly still with a hunger for the game in July that year, he became manager of Newport County in the Southern League. Hollis finally withdrew from football management in 1917, although for a number of years he acted as chairman of Bristol City's shareholders. Sam passed away in Bristol on 17 April 1942.

1897/98

On the departure of Hollis, Woolwich Arsenal appointed the club's first professional secretary-manager for the 1897/98 season: Thomas Brown Mitchell, who was shipped in from Blackburn Rovers.

Mitchell was to remain at Plumstead for less than one season, but he was part of the establishment of professionalism at Woolwich Arsenal. From the Dumfries area of Scotland, Mitchell had crossed the border around 1867 to take up the post of secretary at Leamington Street and then at Ewood Park for about a dozen years.

During Mitchell's short reign, Woolwich Arsenal, bolstered by their best away record as a Football League club, climbed to fifth in their Division, their best ever finish. However, it was still a long way short of the promotion places; eight points above them, Newcastle went up and, a full 10 points better, Burnley won the Division Two Championship. Nevertheless, concluding the season a point higher than Birmingham City and just a point behind Manchester United was more than satisfactory. In the FA Cup, having progressed through three qualifying rounds, beating St Albans 9–0, Sheppy United 3–0 and New Brompton 4–2, Arsenal were knocked out in the first round proper by Burnley (3–1 at Turf Moor).

The toll taken by the long journeys other clubs had to make to get to Plumstead seemed to be proving a distinct advantage for Woolwich who had experienced only 13 home defeats in their first five seasons as a Football League club. However, they had failed to win more than three games on their travels in a single season until 1897/98.

Among the players who joined the club that season were goalkeeper Roger Ord, full-backs Jim McAuley and Alex McConnell, and forwards Fergus Hunt, David Hannah, Bill White and Craig McGeoch, but some of these men, like the manager, lasted only one season in Plumstead.

Although performances improved, attendances, which had been declining over the previous season, continued to fall and the club's financial position became seriously shaky. It seems likely that this situation had an influence on Mitchell's tendering his resignation in March 1898. Later he returned to Blackburn, where he passed away in August 1921, aged 78.

1898/99

Arsenal's 1898/99 campaign was led by George Elcoat from Stockton-on-Tees, who again only lasted a season, but it was enough time for him to continue Mitchell's work of filling the side with Scots. One of their number was John Dick, who was to prove a fine servant of the club at wing-half and as Arsenal's skipper for more than a dozen years.

The League was increased to 18 clubs in this season, and Arsenal's seventh-place finish was a good performance. They were just five points shy of promotion, which was won by Manchester City; Glossop North End, who finished in second place, would return to Division Two the following term.

With Arsenal excused from qualifying rounds, Derby County came to Plumstead in the first round proper of the FA Cup. The team that would finish ninth in Division One that season battered Arsenal 6–0.

Worryingly, Woolwich Arsenal's support was not improving and in an effort to prevent the club from facing bankruptcy, players had to be off-loaded. Elcoat, finding himself in a similar situation to his predecessor, left the Manor Ground at the end of the season.

In the main, Woolwich Arsenal's first years as a Football League club were a struggle in the face of unfavourable location and competition from other professional London clubs. In the last years of the 19th century, the rest of the footballing world's perception of Arsenal had hardly altered from the first days of the club's existence; they were still seen as a hard, uncompromising side and a bit of a nuisance, leaving a trail of injuries wherever they went. No one liked visiting the Manor Ground, and the teams in the Second Division were frustrated as the club consistently kept their head above water.

Arsenal seemed to be the world's most disliked team, but those associated with the Reds became acclimatised to this. Indeed, up to the start of the 20th century, the side's ill-repute developed even more swiftly than the club's arrears. However, the far-reaching consequences of the Boer War between 1899 and 1902 had a huge impact on the Reds, a side that in their first years had a high degree of reliance on the army and the industries that served it. This war effectively robbed Woolwich Arsenal of support as attendances slumped to an average of about 2,000. The custom all over Britain at that time was for people to finish work at Saturday lunchtime (the two-day weekend was still a thing of the future), which would allow time in the pub and a visit to a football match. But, in South London, the Boer War severely curtailed this, as service industries tended to match the demands of the great munitions factory which dominated local commerce. Crucially, Arsenal had introduced a Saturday-afternoon shift to cover the increased demand for their products, so Saturday afternoons for most munitions workers meant compulsory overtime and shift work. Similarly, military personnel, which constituted most of the rest of their supportership, were stationed all over Britain and beyond, either involved directly in the conflict in Africa or acting as cover for regiments fighting the Boers. This situation was to prove nearly as much of a catastrophe for Woolwich Arsenal as it was for the British Army in South Africa.

CHAPTER 11

ENTER THE BRAD

In 1899, Harry Bradshaw took charge of the Arsenal team and he was to be the first really successful manager. He had been appointed secretary of Burnley in 1891, and became chairman two years later. The Turfites, as Burnley were known at that time, were founder members of the Football League and Harry was an influential figure during the League's first years. In 1896, he became Burnley's first team manager, and, although they were relegated from the First Division in his first season, finishing bottom and losing Test Matches (playoffs), Harry immediately led them to promotion and to third place in the First Division the following term (1898/99). That was the club's best ever season in League football and Harry had transformed them into a footballing power.

At the Manor Ground, the Brad (as Harry was known to the Manor Ground faithful) discovered seemingly ever-dwindling attendances with the consequence that the club's best players were sold off to raise the cash for continued survival. It was a recipe for despair.

Born in 1854, Harry never played professionally, but he was a talented administrator and well versed in football strategy. With what small amount of financial resources he was given, Harry initially looked to local talent to boost the side; Archie Cross joined from Dartford and goalkeeper Jimmy Ashcroft came from Gravesend. In 1906, Ashcroft became the club's first England international in a match against Northern Ireland and was selected for all three internationals in 1905/06; he had the enviable gift of being able to punch a ball half the length of the pitch.

Like his predecessors (and many other secretary-managers all over England), Bradshaw looked to Scotland for talent from where he recruited full-backs Jim Jackson and Duncan McNichol. Jackson was an Australian left-back (but with solid Scottish connections) who became the club captain. He was an on-pitch leader, well versed in Aussie-rules 'footie', which proved quite an advantage given the intensely physical nature of the English game at the time. Jim introduced zonal marking to Woolwich and committed himself to controlling everything that his side undertook. His philosophy that he readily shared with his teammates was: 'We're not here to show fancy play. We're here to get points. When we can't get two, we can at least make sure of one.'

Bradshaw fostered the Scottish short, accurate passing game and results gradually improved. By the end of April 1900, the Woolwich side had finished eighth in a league of 18.

In late 1899, the Cup provided a string of encounters with founder members of the Southern League and Kent League neighbours Gillingham-based New Brompton. The saga started in Arsenal's first game of the competition, the third qualifying round, with a 1–1 draw in Plumstead. This was followed by a goalless match in Gillingham, then a 2–2 draw at Millwall's Isle of Dogs ground. The circus moved on to White Hart Lane (which had been Tottenham's home for seven months) where another stalemate was played out, this time 1–1. The matter was finally settled at Gravesend by the only goal of the game and Arsenal were eliminated.

TURN OF THE CENTURY

Football played its millennium trick for the first time when it produced the last games of the 19th century and the first of the 20th century in one season, confusing historians as to which was the last campaign of the 1900s and which was the first of the next century.

By the turn of the century, the Reds had shown themselves to be worthy of the reputation of 'challenging' competitors in the Second Division, and on 12 March 1900 Loughborough, who had inflicted Arsenal's 8–0 record defeat in 1896, came to the Manor Ground to be beaten 12–0. This remains Arsenal's record win and is one of just 18 occasions when a club have scored a dozen times in one Football League game. Having a record win and a record defeat against the same club, a team which left the League as long ago as 1900, with just four years between the results, is, not surprisingly, unmatched, and is quite likely to remain so.

A mere 600 had turned out to watch that record being set, although this was mainly due to the munitions and military work commitments of Arsenal's supporters. However, the number of non-paying spectators also began to increase as people were often unable or unwilling to pay to see just part of a match (for example, if their shift patterns meant they were unable to get to the first part of a match or they had to leave before the end), so they often took to vantage points such as the Southern Outfall Sewer pipe, just as they had done during the club's original tenure at the Manor Ground.

But, in the first full season of the 20th century, Arsenal managed to claim seventh spot in the Second Division. Once more it was a respectable placing, but with 33 points they trailed the League winners Grimsby Town by 13 points (a significant amount at a time when there were only two points awarded for a win). In the Cup, Arsenal travelled to Darwen's Barley Bank ground and beat the Salmoners 2–0 to win the right to entertain First Division Blackburn at the Manor Ground; in what was probably their best result of the season, the Reds cruised to a 2–0 victory. When they were again drawn at home, this time to West Bromwich Albion (who would be relegated that season), hopes were high. But, in a frustrating game that became bogged down in a series of midfield brawls, the Throstles came out the winners by the only goal of the game.

With crowds now averaging around the 6,000 mark, Woolwich Arsenal became the best-supported club in the Second Division. Good results had drawn decent crowds, and as such financial worries, along with the shadow of the Boer War, began to recede.

The following campaign saw Arsenal achieve their highest-ever placing in football. Although they finished nine points from promotion, only West Bromwich Albion, Middlesbrough (who were elected to the League the previous season) and Preston North End were placed above them (a better goal average would have pushed the Reds into third). The Cup offered up a home draw with Luton Town (who were the first team in Southern England to openly make professional payments in 1886). The Reds' 2–0 victory brought Newcastle to Plumstead, where the Magpies achieved a comfortable 2–0 win.

Woolwich went one better in 1902/03, finishing third, just three points adrift of Birmingham City and promotion. Manchester City were the Champions. Woolwich were four points clear of Bristol City, and, as such, showed themselves to be the top Southern club and a clearly better side than Manchester United, who were back in fifth place.

A creditable away draw against Brentford brought the Bees over to Plumstead for a 5–0 drubbing in the Cup, but the holders Sheffield United, who had finished fourth in the First Division, just three points off the League Champions, had no trouble at the Manor Ground and took the game 3–1. In that match, played on a mound-like pitch, the goalkeepers could not see each other, and, bizarrely, nor could the linesmen.

But improvements in support culminated in a crowd of more than 25,000 at this match and receipts for the game were a satisfying £1,000; this was the first time Arsenal had passed the four-figure mark for takings from one match.

CHAPTER 12
PROMOTION

1903/04

In their 1903/04 campaign, Woolwich Arsenal achieved what just a few years earlier had seemed impossible: they became the first Southern club to be promoted to the First Division.

Arsenal were now becoming known as the Gunners, following the ordnance factory's heightened profile during the Boer War; although it had been applied for some years, the name had not been favoured over the 'Reds'.

The Gunners had needed a single point from their last match of the season, a home game against Port Vale, and they had done just just enough with a goalless draw. Just one point behind the mighty Preston North End, the South Londoners won the runners-up spot in the League, on 49 points, one clear of Manchester United who remained in the Second Division. Of their 36 games Woolwich had lost only six and won 21.

An outstanding home record had been the basis of Arsenal's success, with an excellent goal average of 67 to 5. Not a match was lost at the Manor Ground (only two points were dropped when the last two home games were drawn). Burton United and Leicester Fosse were both beaten 8–0. Away from Plumstead, the Gunners managed just half-a-dozen victories, but, with 91 goals scored and only 22 conceded, the club had achieved their best ever season in terms of results (although, naturally, it is hard to evaluate seasons with different numbers of games).

Jimmy Ashcroft played in every match. Other consistent members of the team included local Dartford man Archie Cross; skipper Jimmy Jackson; John Dick; the amateur Percy Sands, who was a schoolteacher in Woolwich; left-half Roddy McEachrane from Inverness, a tidy, thoughtful player; Tommy Briercliffe (who had been signed from

Blackburn Rovers); John Coleman; centre-forward Bill Gooing (a reliable goalscorer, who was ever present in the promotion side); and Bill Linward, who came to Plumstead from West Ham.

But a great deal was owed to Tommy Shanks, Arsenal's and the League's leading scorer, with 24 goals. No Arsenal player would accomplish this feat again until Ted Drake in the 1934/35 season, and the first post-war Arsenal player to repeat this achievement was Ronnie Rooke during the 1947/48 campaign.

Woolwich's best ever League season was complemented by a decent performance in the Cup, after taking three tries to beat Bristol Rovers (the West Countrymen were finally defeated by a single goal at White Hart Lane). Fulham were also beaten 1–0 at the Manor Ground but Manchester City came to South London to knock Arsenal out in the second round, winning the tie easily (2–0).

It was clear to the club committee that promotion would mean bigger crowds and as such the capacity of the Manor Ground had to be increased. In 1904, huge, steeply banked terraced areas were constructed at the west and south ends of the ground, largely to block the view from the sewer bank in an attempt to put a stop to the free viewing area for those game enough to brave the sewer pipe. This meant that over 25,000 would be able to watch Arsenal, although crowds of 20,000 and 30,000 had been squeezed in even before these improvements.

The large earth terraces probably reminded many of the Gunners' soldier supporters (who could make up half the Manor Ground crowds at this time) of Spion Kop, a hill in Natal that was the site of one of the most awful battles of the Boer War in which hundreds of British soldiers had been slaughtered in crowded trenches. And the embankment, which was nicknamed after this bloodied hill, then became known to locals as just 'the Kop'; soon many of the greatest terraced areas throughout the Football League (most famously Anfield) also came to be known as the Kop.

Woolwich Arsenal used 20 players during their promotion campaign, only two of whom had been with the club prior to the coming of Harry Bradshaw. Harry had put Arsenal on the big-time football map and it therefore caused quite a sensation when, in April 1904, before the Reds' debut season in the top flight, he gave up the prospect of First Division football at Plumstead and moved to Craven Cottage; lured by way of a large salary, he became Fulham's first manager. Fulham were newly formed as a company and played in the First Division of the Southern League.

Over five years, Harry had transformed the fortunes of the club, taking them from the verge of bankruptcy and building a successful team which won promotion to the First Division. He had overseen continued improvements in play and results, and the resultant increase in support; with the club able to afford new players, Bradshaw had acquired the likes of Roddy McEachrane and a complete forward line of Tom Briercliffe, John Coleman, Bill Gooing, Tom Shanks and Bill Linward.

During the early part of the Brad's reign at the Manor Ground (1901), Tottenham had won the FA Cup to become the first non-League club (after the introduction of the Football League) to achieve this feat (an estimated 20,000 packed the streets to welcome Spurs home). At the time, it had looked as if London neighbours Arsenal would be very much the poor relations as it seemed it was all they could do to survive their financial struggle.

But the team Bradshaw built were able to remain in

the top flight for a creditable nine years, pushing as high as sixth place (with 14 victories and 10 draws in their 38 games). However, only once in those nine First Division seasons, between 1904 and 1913, did they win more League games than they lost.

Bradshaw's two sons, William and Joseph, had been players with Woolwich Arsenal and they followed him to Fulham. (Joe would also follow his father to become the manager of Fulham.)

Within the space of two seasons, Harry led Fulham to two successive Southern League Championships and election into the Football League for the 1907/08 season. In their first term among the elite of English football, Fulham finished fourth (just three points short of promotion) and reached the semi-final of the FA Cup.

During 1905, needing to rise to the competition threatened by the newly developed Stamford Bridge and Chelsea FC, the Brad saw the redevelopment of Craven Cottage, with the temporary structures (known as the Rabbit Hutch stand) making way for the Stevenage Road stand.

Harry's role, like most of his peers in football management at the time, was mostly administrative. Day to day, trainers worked with the players and, while there were recognised strategies of play, there wasn't the specialist coaching or advanced tactical analysis of modern football. Improvisation and a rudimentary team structure, often based on military models, were worked out in the main by players with the odd encouraging word from trainers and managers about 'attitude' and 'deportment'. But the astute choice of the players Bradshaw brought to Craven Cottage and the Manor Ground shows him to have been a shrewd judge of how football players fit together as units of a team.

While with Fulham, the Brad continued to plunder Scottish talent, as he had at Woolwich Arsenal, favouring the close-control, dribbling and passing skills exhibited north of the border. Like Arsène Wenger in later years, Harry was unafraid and swift to make what he saw as necessary alterations, even to winning teams, and in his half-decade in control at Craven Cottage he selected 69 players for his first teams; he never deployed less than 21 in any season.

However, Fulham's 1908/09 campaign did not meet his high expectations and, after his five-year contract expired, Harry became secretary of the Southern League, a position he held until 1921 when he took his retirement, and he passed away three years later in September 1924.

The Brad remains one of the most influential managers Arsenal have known.

CHAPTER 13

TOP-FLIGHT GUNNERS

1904/05

Phil Kelso was appointed as Harry Bradshaw's successor and became Arsenal's first manager in the top flight. Born in 1871, at Largs, on the Firth of Clyde, Kelso was a tough, pragmatic and craggy Scotsman, who for many years had been associated with Hibernian FC and was among the best-known men in the Scottish game. An austere and often bad-tempered man, Kelso always remained detached from the players he managed. He made it his first priority to strengthen the Arsenal forward line, signing Charlie Satterthwaite, Tom Fitchie and Bob Templeton, and, later, Bill Garbutt and Bert Freeman.

Satterthwaite (whose brother Joe, eight years Charlie's junior, also played for Woolwich in 1907 at inside-left) was a popular player among the Gunners fans. His shooting, with his 16 stone of force behind it, produced some momentous results; he once smashed the stanchion with one of his cannon-like drives and in a match against Sheffield United a 25-yard shot hit the Blades' bar, bounced back, knocked the keeper unconscious and still rebounded into the net. Kelso also shored up the defence with Scottish full-backs Archie Gray and Jim Sharp (in much the same way as other Arsenal managers of the future, it seems Phil had a penchant for his own countrymen). Jim Buchan, Jim Bigden and John Hunter had also come into the Arsenal side that had won promotion.

Kelso had come to a club that seemed to have a future. The debut season in the First Division was of course Woolwich Arsenal's greatest achievement to that point, and at first attendances were good, up to 25,000 at times, and season-ticket holders were encouraged (for a time, the Reds had more season-ticket holders than any other club in England).

Arsenal's opening game was at St James' Park. Newcastle were well acclimatised to life in the First Division, having taken their place in the top flight in

1898, and the Magpies would claim their first League Championship in April 1905.

The Tynesiders introduced full-back Bill McCracken, an Irish international who would later became infamous for his management of the offside trap. Jackie Rutherford and Bob Templeton were flankmen for the North Easterners, both of whom would play for Woolwich Arsenal (although not at the same time).

In the first 45 minutes, the visitors played well enough and for some time it looked like being a close match. But Arsenal didn't take advantage of the opportunities they created in the early part of the game.

The roaring start had a cost that was plain to see as the Londoners' energy dissipated. Gradually, the Magpies began to dominate, playing surprisingly good football for the opening match of the season, and, thanks to Rutherford, who scored directly from a corner kick, the home side went into the break with a one-goal lead.

In the second half, Ron Orr converted following a Templeton free-kick. Orr doubled his tally to make Newcastle comfortable winners.

The teams were:

NEWCASTLE UNITED: Charlie Watts, Bill McCracken, Andy McCombie, Alec Gardner, Andy Aitken, Jack Carr, Jackie Rutherford, Jim Howie, Bill Appleyard, Ron Orr, Bob Templeton

WOOLWICH ARSENAL: Jim Ashcroft, Archie Gray, Jim Jackson, John Dick, Jim Buchan, Jim Bigden, Tom Briercliffe, John Coleman, Bill Gooing, John Hunter, Charlie Satterthwaite

Arsenal's first victory among the football elite of England was a 2–0 result against Wolverhampton Wanderers at the Manor Ground on 24 September 1904 (Satterthwaite and Coleman were the first Gunners to score in a First Division match). Although the Woolwich side finished in the bottom half of the table (10th out of 18), their dozen victories kept them safe from the threat of relegation.

The FA Cup had been a bit of an anticlimax; in two games with Bristol City, one goal eliminated Arsenal.

However, one of the most groundbreaking games played at the Manor Ground that season was Arsenal's first international game. As a club, Woolwich Arsenal recognised that competition between clubs from different countries would attract crowds, and a team made up of players from several clubs in Paris were invited to play in Plumstead. The visitors didn't seem to like the weather and their football talents left much to be desired. Indeed, they turned up one short and Titus Hodge, an Arsenal reserve, had to 'guest' for the French in order for them to field a full team.

The match took place on a damp 5 December 1904 afternoon in front of a crowd of about 3,000. The Gunners hit the rigging 26 times, while the Parisians replied with a single goal (scored by Hodge as the home defence opened to allow him through). The *Daily Express* told the tale: 'Football as played at Plumstead yesterday, although highly amusing, serves no good purpose beyond the fact that it proves to our friends from across the Channel that they still have a lot to learn before they can hope to compete with our best Association clubs ... Such farces are seldom seen on English grounds, and it is to be hoped that in future fixtures of this kind will not be encouraged. Any one of our school XIs would easily have given the Paris team of yesterday a beating.'

1905/06

The 1905/06 season was to start well for Woolwich Arsenal with a 3–1 home victory over Liverpool, the side that would claim the League Championship that term. But there were only three more wins in the League for the Gunners before Christmas Day when, taking the centre-forward role, Andy Ducat claimed a hat-trick in his debut for Woolwich against Newcastle United. It was exceptionally sad that, like many of Andy's peers, his best playing years would be lost to the Great War.

The Gunners' breakthrough that season came in the FA Cup in which the club pushed beyond the second round for the first time in their 20-year history to reach the semi-finals via a demanding route; West Ham were beaten in East London following a draw at the Manor Ground; Watford were defeated 3–0; Sunderland, a side that had been League Champions four times, were thrashed 5–0, an amazing result at that time. Plumstead-born Charlie Buchan, Gunner immortal of the future, later wrote that he sold one of his school books to pay for his admission to that Sunderland match, for which he later received a severe beating. (Of course, he had no way of knowing as he stood crushed into the Manor Ground with

30,000 others that he was watching the two clubs with whom he would become a star of the game.)

The quarter-final matched Arsenal with Manchester United at Bank Street. A 3–2 win sent the Londoners to meet Newcastle United at Stoke's Victoria Ground (which the Potters had called home since 1878 – they stayed there for a record 119 years, which remains unmatched by any English club).

Between 1905 and 1911, the mighty Magpies would appear in five FA Cup Finals. Arsenal had sent out one of their finest ever forward lines for the demanding tie and, when the game was still young, Bert Freeman, looking sharp at centre-forward, hit the Newcastle bar. But, with goals from the great Colin Veitch and Jimmy Howie, the Magpies beat the Gunners 2–0 to go through to the 35th FA Cup Final.

The trophy was won (for the first time) by Everton at Crystal Palace in front of 75,609 spectators. Sandy Young, who later turned out for Spurs, scored the only goal of the game in the 75th minute to send Newcastle back to the North East a disappointed side.

Arsenal's wingers would both go on to be international players. On the right, Bill Garbutt would be capped by England after he had joined Blackburn Rovers. The capricious Scotsman Bobby Templeton who raided down the left flank won caps while with Aston Villa and Newcastle. A mercurial defender, Bob, a hairdresser in the 'real world', was able to bend the ball viciously, a rare talent in those days. (He is unhappily probably best remembered for the 1902 Ibrox disaster. During the game there between England and Scotland, Templeton had started on one of his many twisting runs down the wing. The great crowd on his side of the pitch pressed forward to take in the spectacle and it was this shift that caused a wooden stand to sway and give way; 25 people were killed as they fell through the structure to the ground.)

Woolwich hung on to Bert Freeman for a couple of years, but, like so many quality players that came through the Arsenal ranks, he had to be sold eventually.

Off the field, many of the Woolwich men were recognised as great 'social animals' around the Plumstead district. For instance, Templeton and Bill Gooing often instigated singing in the local hostelries and were not hard to persuade when it came to knocking out a jig on bar tables. The *Kentish Independent* once reported how, to the amazement of many a witness, the pair convinced the Mayor of Woolwich to join them in a close-harmony rendition of a locally well-known music hall ditty of the time,

'Football's For Me'. One journalist (paraphrasing the nursery rhyme) wrote of Templeton, a temperamental, unpredictable player, not immune from missing the odd training session, 'When he's good, he's very good. When he's bad, he's horrid.'

Arsenal concluded their second season of competing against the cream of football in a mediocre 12th place in Division One, but, although Bristol City won Division Two, there was no other Southern club that could match their prowess.

TOP OF THE LEAGUE

As is nearly always the case, performances matched the level of support. In the 1906/07 season, Arsenal took 15 points from their opening nine games and became the first Southern club ever to head the First Division.

The South Londoners were to make the semi-final of the Cup for the second consecutive season. Their route to the last four was just as demanding as the previous year. Victories against Grimsby, Bristol City (who at that point were lying second in the First Division), Bristol Rovers and Barnsley set up a confrontation with the powerful Wednesday at St Andrew's. One of the Wednesday forwards that day was Harry Chapman, brother of Herbert, the great Arsenal manager of the 1930s.

The Woolwich lads took the lead after just 10 minutes' play, when Garbutt headed in a Satterthwaite cross. Then came disaster; Ashcroft, Arsenal's goalkeeper, collided with centre-forward Dave Wilson, while rushing out of his area to collect a loose ball (then keepers were allowed to handle anywhere in their own half; it wasn't until 1912 that the FA ruled that they would only be allowed to handle the ball in their own penalty area). Ashcroft was badly injured and, from the resulting free-kick that the referee, Jack Howcroft (whose brother Harry had played for Bolton Wanderers), inexplicably awarded Wednesday, the Sheffield side pulled level.

The incident changed the whole character of the game. Wednesday scored two more to go through to the Final against Everton, while Arsenal had to wait another 20 years before they won a semi-final (when they defeated Southampton 2–1 at Stamford Bridge but the Gunners lost in the Final at Wembley to Cardiff City by the only goal of the game).

Everton were looking to win two Cups in a row, but a crowd of 84,584 saw the Sheffield side go 1–0 up after 21 minutes via a goal from Jimmy Stewart. Jack

Sharp drew the Toffees level seven minutes before half-time but a last-minute goal from George Simpson stopped the Liverpool Blues from becoming the first team since Blackburn Rovers in 1891 to retain the trophy. This was Wednesday's second Cup Final win, following their 2–1 defeat of Wolverhampton Wanderers in 1896.

At the end of the 1906/07 season, the Plumstead lads went on a 16-day tour of Europe, playing eight games, and winning all but one. It was the Gunners' first trip abroad. A Belgium XI were beaten in Brussels 2–1 and The Hague were defeated 6–3. Preussen (Prussia) were taken apart 9–1 in Berlin before two games against SK Slavia IPS ended in 7–5 and 4–2 victories. The tour was rounded off with a couple of games against Budapest which concluded in a 9–0 win and a 2–2 draw.

It had been a very successful season for the Reds, and many hoped that it was perhaps a promise of things to come. Finishing seventh in the First Division was another improvement and the team generally impressed with their well-organised play. The reserve side won the London League and the South Eastern League. John 'Tim' Coleman had played at inside-right for England and full-back Jimmy Sharp, who had captained Scotland in 1904, twice represented his country (4 March in a 1–0 defeat by the Welsh at the Racecourse Ground, Wrexham, and on 6 April in a 1–1 draw with England at St James' Park).

However, it was Bristol City, now back in the top flight, who finished runners-up to Newcastle United, and took the plaudits as the South's top club.

CHAPTER 14

TROUBLED
TIMES

1907/08

There were great hopes at the Manor Ground as
September 1907 opened its doors for business. But an
opening home draw with Notts County, three straight
defeats and only one win in the first seven games did
not bode well and it became clear that the previous
season was as good as things were going to get for
Woolwich Arsenal for a while. As results faltered and
it seemed attendances had passed their peak, old
worries remerged.

But at least troubles were forgotten for the day on
7 November 1907, King Edward VII's birthday. The
event was celebrated at the Royal Arsenal works by

giving everyone the day off. And the Reds scheduled their first all-London clash in the First Division with a match against Chelsea at Stamford Bridge. The Gunners won 2–1 to the delight of the huge Arsenal contingent among the 65,000 crowd that crossed London to see the game.

Woolwich was still not an easy place to reach, and certainly other London clubs were more accessible. Big-spending Chelsea, who had entered the First Division, presented Arsenal with their first real 'local' competitor since the club had joined the Football League. But, as well as the Pensioners, there was an abundance of football to watch, including the expanding Southern League.

Arsenal's support and finances were not of sufficient strength to endure a downturn in on-field performance, and it now appeared as if there were as many difficulties off the pitch as there were on it. An early exit from the Cup, being forced to replay a first-round home draw with Hull and losing 4–1 after the long trip to Yorkshire, together with unconvincing League form, led Phil Kelso to resign early in 1908, by which time it had become clear that he was not in the same league as Harry Bradshaw in terms of his management ability.

Before the end of the season, he had returned to Scotland to run a hotel in Largs.

But later, in 1909, he became yet another former Arsenal manager to take up a similar post with Fulham, stepping into Bradshaw's shoes. The migration across London from Woolwich to SW6 would eventually amount to nine of the first 14 Fulham managers having either played for or managed the Reds.

Like Bradshaw, Kelso was an administrator, never having played professionally (but on one occasion during a wartime emergency he did turn out for Fulham – he was 47 at the time). At Craven Cottage, he was obliged to deal with a series of financial challenges, but succeeded in keeping the team in the Second Division throughout his time with the club, although it was touch and go in his last season; a 1–0 home win in Kelso's final game in charge kept Fulham up by the skin of their teeth.

Kelso made some good signings and he developed two useful teams, on either side of World War I. Like Bradshaw, he favoured the close-passing game, seen very much as a Scottish genre, although he never even got a sniff of promotion.

Kelso was big on discipline and was outspoken about smoking and drinking. He liked his players to reside in or near London but insisted on their getting together outside the city the night before games. Several players left the club due to his stern regimen.

He would remain at Craven Cottage throughout World War I and after, until his retirement in 1924. As a manager with sole control of team affairs for 15 years, he remains the longest-serving Fulham boss, with four seasons of League football lost during the First World War.

His final years at the Cottage were soured by a bribery scandal. Kelso was 53 when he left football, but he remained in the Fulham district, becoming the landlord of The Grove in Hammersmith before moving to the Rising Sun in the Fulham Road (coincidentally where Gus Mears had laid his plans to start Chelsea in 1905).

An enthusiastic golfer and bowls player, Kelso served as chairman of the Football League Managers and Secretaries Association, before he died in February 1935 aged 64.

MORRELL AT THE MANOR

Following Kelso's departure, George Morrell took over at the Manor Ground to become the fifth Arsenal secretary-manager in a decade, arriving at

Plumstead at the start of what was to be one of the most crucial times in the club's history.

A muscular Glaswegian, born around 1873, George started his managerial career at an early age, as a committee member of Glenure Athletic, a junior club in Glasgow. He went on to become secretary, treasurer and president and an occasional player for the side. He moved to Glasgow Rangers at a time when the club were fighting for survival but over two or three years he worked to restore the Gers' fortunes.

Morrell qualified and practised as a referee and in 1905 was appointed from a list of 85 applicants as secretary-manager of Greenock Morton, a club that was also deeply in debt. Morrell helped 'the pride of the Clyde' get themselves back in the black and was pivotal in getting the club elected into the Scottish First Division.

Arriving at Woolwich Arsenal in February 1908, Morrell was once more confronted with a team lacking appropriate support and the associated financial problems. But he was regarded as being financially brilliant in the football arena. He had almost single-handedly turned around the fortunes of two clubs in seemingly impossible positions; why could he not do the same for Arsenal?

Initially, Morrell was tasked with achieving results on the field, but the club couldn't meet their wage bill. During 1907/08, Arsenal averaged about 10,000 for each home League game. Chelsea, with better access to their ground (and a better ground generally), attracted nearly three times that number. Morrell was obliged to sell some of the Gunners' most influential players, and, within a few months, John Coleman, Bert Freeman, Peter Kyle, Jimmy Sharp, Jimmy Ashcroft and Billy Garbutt had left Woolwich Arsenal.

(After leaving Woolwich for Blackburn Rovers, Bill Garbutt was coaching with Genoa in 1914. His club won the Italian League the following year. By 1927, he was in Rome, and two years later he had joined Naples. In 1935/36, Bill coached the Spanish Champions Athletic Bilbao, but the coming of the Spanish Civil War obliged him to return to Italy. During World War II, Garbutt, helped by friends, went into hiding, but in 1946 he returned to Genoa. Bert Freeman moved from Plumstead to Everton and led the Football League's goalscorers three times between 1908 and 1913. He won an FA Cup winner's medal in 1914, scoring the only goal of the game for Burnley against Liverpool.)

Arsenal finished the season equal 14th with Blackburn Rovers, trailing fellow Londoners, new boys Chelsea. It was just not good enough. Morrell would have to improve things, or more than his job would be on the line: the very viability of the club was threatened.

Morrell's first full term as manager started on 2 September 1908. The editor of the inaugural programme of the new season forthright on the subject of the club losing their star players, declaring, 'Here we go again ... and the followers of Arsenal look forward to the advent of another season with a great number of the players on whom we rely practically unknown quantities. The "Reds" will look somewhat strange without such faces as Ashcroft, Sharp, Coleman, Freeman, Kyle and Garbutt but we believe capable men have been engaged to replace them and we look forward to a successful season.'

As the old Gypsy saying has it, hope is the last thing to die, but it was almost 20 years before the Gunners had another season to rival the two that started in 1905.

The editor went on, 'If we do not have a back of the same calibre as Sharp, we have one likely to prove a worthy successor in the person of [Joseph] Shaw.'

The club managed to reach a respectable (and somewhat surprising) sixth position in the League and reclaim their mastery of the South (Chelsea finished in 11th place). This was quite an achievement given the fact that the club had to compensate for the loss of so many good players.

Arguably, the best of all the Arsenal players before the move to Highbury was right-half Andy Ducat, who began to flower that season (although he had been a potent presence since coming into the side) and he had a lot to do with the Gunners' commendable performance. Andy was a constructive half-back, who scored three goals on his first appearance for Arsenal in 1905. He was selected for all three home internationals for England during the 1909/10 season at the tender age of 23, and in all he played six times for his country over a period of 11 years (this was at a time when a man in his mid-twenties was young for an international and when the home countries could expect to play just three games a season). He was sold to Aston Villa for £1,500 in 1912. Ducat was the first of several footballer-cricketers (he turned out for both Surrey, alongside Jack Hobbs and Tom Hayward, and England) who have played for Arsenal. Denis

Compton is certainly the most famous cricketer ever to be on their books but the club's former chairman Samuel Hill-Wood played county cricket for Derbyshire against the MCC at Lords in 1900. He scored 10 runs off one ball, which is still the highest-recorded score from a single delivery.

In the FA Cup that season, Arsenal managed to get past Croydon Common after a replay, and a massive 32,000 packed into the Manor Ground to see the next-round game against Millwall Athletic in February 1909.

The *Kentish Mercury* reported on the encounter with the Lions, whose fans had made their way to Plumstead in huge swarms, using a wide variety of means to get to the game. Special trains, trams, buses, traps and steamboats had been laid on. (Bizarrely, my grandfather recalled the vision of six Millwall supporters whom he identified by their blue and white top hats unicycling through Plumstead.)

There still wasn't a straightforward or direct route to get to the ground, despite the fact that the train station was directly opposite the Arsenal home. Services were irregular and unreliable, although important matches were facilitated by special services. Getting into the ground was one thing, getting out after the 1–1 draw was quite another. It was rumoured that some Millwall fans just about made it back to Dog Island for the replay four days later to watch their team win the tie by the only goal.

1909/10

The 1909/10 season was five games old before Woolwich Arsenal finally walked off a football pitch as winners, having defeated Chelsea 3–2 at Plumstead. But four more defeats followed before Everton were beaten 1–0 at the Manor Ground. Arsenal just about avoided relegation, finishing two points clear of Chelsea who went down with Bolton Wanderers. In effect, their 11 April 1–0 win over Aston Villa (who were to be the League Champions that term, and who had thrashed the Gunners 5–1 on the opening day of the campaign) saved the Gunners' season. That match had been replayed after the abandonment of the fixture early in September 1909 after 80 minutes' play.

Tottenham had entered Division One by way of promotion in 1909 and became the new masters of the South, despite finishing 15th. Arsenal had taken three points out of four from the North Londoners that term, winning the first League meeting between the two clubs on 4 December that year 1–0 at the Manor Ground.

The FA Cup did little to raise morale. Arsenal were beaten 5–0 in the second round at Goodison Park which blotted out the memory of their 3–0 defeat of Watford in the previous tie.

The team's performances looked conspicuously pedestrian and their reputation for 'strong play' was being reinvigorated. But Joe Shaw, a reliable defender, stayed loyal to Arsenal and, with a playing career of 15 years, became a stalwart and long-term servant of the club. Eventually he would become assistant manager.

Woolwich Arsenal had not been able to recover from the seeming fire sale that started in 1908. Ashcroft, their reliable keeper, was particularly missed. Crowds dwindled, as the results failed to come. By 1910, the club were £3,000 in debt, in effect bankrupt and up for sale, and relegation threatened.

CHAPTER 15

SIR HENRY NORRIS

During March 1910, Woolwich Arsenal went into voluntary administration; the club's debts amounted to £12,500. Mr Brannan, the administrator, was tasked to sell off Woolwich Arsenal's assets to pay off the club's creditors (although the only asset of any real value was the Manor Ground). Brannan sold everything to a consortium of small businessmen led by George Leavey, who had been part of Woolwich Arsenal for a number of years. He had no official position within the club but had often helped out with cash drawn from his personal resources.

In May, wanting Arsenal to survive, the consortium offered shares for general sale. The majority of these were subscribed to by William Hall and Henry Norris, who each bought 240 shares (a 37.5 per cent stake, the controlling interest of the company), giving the pair more than a third of the total shares on offer. This acquisition was the start of the road to Highbury.

Other prominent shareholders included Leavey himself, who purchased 100 shares and Tottenham Hotspur FC, who reportedly bought the same number, which they consequently sold prior to the new football season. Not one of the original founders of the club acquired shares, and so any remaining solid connection with the club's first days and Dial Square was lost to commercial necessity.

As such, from around 1910, the history of Arsenal is dominated by things happening off the field rather than on it. It also began to revolve around the powerful character of Henry Norris, who, while Woolwich Arsenal were making their first marks in the Football League, had been the chairman of Fulham and had financed much of the development at Craven Cottage.

Born in 1865, Henry Norris was to become one of the most powerful figures in football by the start of the 20th century. There are those who have thought of him as the stereotypical Edwardian scoundrel and he has been described as the archetypal despot figure of the game, cold as steel and hard as a stone. It has been suggested that his equivalent in the contemporary popular mind might include Terry Brown, Robert Maxwell, Ken Bates and Doug Ellis (although this is unfair to him and them). But some might detect echoes of his approach to football in the likes of Roman Abramovich and he might even be seen as the first 'Football Tsar' recognisable in the modern game. There is a strong case for claiming that his interventions gave us the modern incarnations of Arsenal, Chelsea and Fulham, clubs that themselves have gone a long way to saving other teams from extinction over the years. In many ways, the Premier League could be seen to be partly a legacy of the activity of Henry Norris.

Brought up in a working-class family, Norris was always ambitious. He had attended a minor public school, but, as he was to admit, 'school was not for me'; he detested authority figures and time-wasters. Norris largely ran things his way. As a 14-year-old, his first job was with a modest local solicitors practice. For a year he read articles but seemingly in need of something more 'dynamic' he moved into the building industry. It seems Henry learned to charm when necessary, to get customers and opponents to be convinced of and adopt his perspective, some enthusiastically, others grudgingly and not a few as part of accepting the fait accompli. As a successful estate agent, Norris became notorious as a man who got his own way. One of his competitors in the foggy world of the Edwardian building trade once implied that Norris effectively ran a protection racket to promote his business, although the swift threat of legal action brought a retraction. It seems he was a man to be feared as much as respected and soon it was recognised that no one crossed Henry Norris.

During 1910, Norris capitalised on Arsenal's problems to take over the Manor Ground club. The Woolwich board welcomed him with open arms, aware of his political 'dexterity' and how he had led Fulham's almost implausible rise through the Southern League and into the Second Division of the Football League in a mere four years. This impressive feat seemed to invite whispers that large sums of money may have assisted the Cottagers' ascent to the heady heights of English football, but there was no definite evidence to back up the rumours.

Nevertheless, Fulham undoubtedly quickly became a footballing power after Norris took over as their chairman and their record was impressive. In 1902/03, the Cottagers won promotion to the Southern League First Division and the club were converted into a limited liability company. With Norris now on the Fulham Ltd board, they won that League in 1906 and 1907.

Former Arsenal manager Harry Bradshaw's leadership had been behind much of this success but the club's immediate admission to the Football League on application demonstrated Henry Norris's much-faceted influence, especially in terms of the Football League. In the 1907 election, the Cottagers easily topped the poll (28 votes) to replace Burton United.

Norris was recognised as 'a self-made man'. His 'empire' was Southwest London and he made his money in the property market. His company Allen & Norris interacted between the building and banking industries and he developed a complex network of contacts through which he helped to produce the expansive Southwest London suburb of Fulham from its formerly rural base (he was directly responsible for building over 2,000 houses in Fulham and had a hand in many more developments in the district).

Much of this activity was similar to that of his rival

and contemporary at Chelsea, Gus Mears, but Norris went further. Having observed the expansion of the building industry and the need to provide homes for the exploding population of London, Norris moved into real estate, extending his business network to local authorities and government; his reputation as someone not to cross swords with was enhanced. He reputedly amassed favours and knowledge about the professional and private lives of those he came across in the course of the wealth-building activities that dominated his waking hours. While there is no evidence of any actual wrongdoing, his connections extended both up and down the social scale; annoying bureaucratic obstacles that held others back did not seem to deter Norris.

Norris was Mayor of Fulham from 1909 for seven years, and in 1917 he received a Knighthood. A member of the Conservative & Unionist party, he went on to become MP for East Fulham in 1918, a tenure that was to last until 1922.

To call Norris an 'autocratic character' probably understates his general deportment. Bernard Joy, a class amateur for Arsenal, who became a revered journalist, said of Norris that he was 'nothing less than a dictator' and indeed he approached football as a cut-throat business. His management style was tenaciously authoritarian and he was by most accounts a frightening man. An almost emaciated figure, over six feet in height (very tall for that era) and almost constantly sucking on a pipe (sometimes unlit and/or unloaded), he looked down on his competitors in every way. A dapper dresser, Norris liked trench coats and a crisp, starched white shirt. He was never seen out without an expensive if sober bowler hat perched on his head.

His superior demeanour was emphasised by his habit of glaring at those he came across through his pince-nez (spectacles, popular in the 19th century, which are supported without earpieces, by pinching the bridge of the nose). The lenses were so thick that it was sometimes hard to know who he was looking at. Almost hidden behind his walrus moustache, Norris would not countenance criticism and received advice as insult.

But he was both persuasive and influential. Over the years, he cultivated close associations with members of the LMC, principally with Liverpool's Irish John McKenna, its president. As an MP, Norris chose to support what he portrayed as the interests of football, particularly when they coincided with his own, but he did this successfully, and, while many recognised his focused self-interest, they also understood that they too could and did benefit.

Leslie Knighton, an Arsenal manager while Norris was chairman of the club between 1919 and 1925, in his autobiography said of Norris, 'I soon found out that everyone was afraid of Sir Henry. And no wonder! I have never met his equal for logic, invective and ruthlessness against all who opposed him. When I disagreed with him at board meetings and had to stand up for what I knew was best for the club, he used to flay me with words until I was reduced to fuming, helpless silence. Then, as I sat not knowing what to say, and trying to bottle up what I was tempted to say, he would whip round and shout: "Well Knighton, we pay you a great deal of money to advise us and all you do is sit there as if you were dumb".'

But later Knighton wrote, 'Sir Henry would ask my advice, smile, wheedle ... and I was falling over myself to help him again. He did it with everyone. Those board meetings took years off my life.'

Similar to a group of influential Londoners of the Edwardian era from humble backgrounds, Norris was aware that London seemed unable to match the

Midlands and the North in what was the national winter sport and, probably seeing the considerable market opportunity this represented, he resolved to build a London-based club with the capacity to compete with the best of the rest.

As the centre of Norris's business and other interests were in Fulham, it made sense to start his efforts in that area. However, by 1908, it seems he had understood that his Craven Cottage outpost was unlikely to be a powerbase of the type he needed to dominate football. While Fulham had done well, like Woolwich Arsenal, they could not boast the support that the big clubs in Britain were commanding at that time (many tens of thousands were attending games at Northern clubs).

By 1910, Fulham had what was for the time a substantial overdraft (more than £3,000), while Arsenal were down and practically out financially. This was when Norris took over at the Manor Ground, although he continued to be a Fulham director until the First World War. His fellow director at Plumstead, William Hall, was also Fulham chairman up to the same period and the two men clearly controlled both Fulham and Arsenal. It was, at least in part, because of this that the League was to later resolve that no one individual could have a controlling interest in more than one League club.

It seems Norris had turned his attentions to Woolwich Arsenal for a number of reasons. He was unlikely to be able to get the better of Charlie Roberts at Tottenham or Gus Mears at Chelsea who had their own ambitions, which were probably similar to those that Norris fostered. Although he did try to colonise Stamford Bridge in 1905, he soon realised Mears would not be easily moved from the club he had virtually created. The most obvious incentives for Norris to make a move on Arsenal were the club's dire financial situation and the Gunners' relatively weak fan base. He had, of course, recruited two former Woolwich managers, both of whom had joined Fulham because they knew that the Manor Ground team had gone about as far as they could at the time, given their general profile and prospects. So it is likely that Norris had some strategy for change in mind before he actually attempted to take over the club; it seems he was merely waiting for things to hit rock bottom, which as a seasoned property speculator would have been second nature to him.

But Woolwich Arsenal were a First Division club and fitted the investment profile, in terms of building a foundation that offered a conduit to the potential financial rewards of mass football support of the Northern variety. Norris could have gone for West Ham or Orient and spent years having to play political and social games to gain access to this 'market', but Arsenal already owned their 'pitch' and that made them unique in London, as Chelsea and Tottenham were clearly not for sale. No doubt, Norris would have realised that the club would need to move away from Plumstead, which did not seem likely to become a hotbed of football support in the foreseeable future.

Norris had evidently not acted in haste and had been watching things develop at Arsenal for some time; the club did not have the kind of entrepreneurial clout that Tottenham, Chelsea and Fulham had to guide them and as such they were always going to be a relatively 'soft touch' for the likes of Norris, although he also may not have fancied taking on Danskin and Humble. So it wasn't until the summer of 1910, as Arsenal just managed to dodge relegation, that Norris finally made his move after the two great founders and protectors of the embryonic Gunners had left the proverbial central stage.

His original idea was to merge Woolwich Arsenal

with Fulham and move the new club to Craven Cottage with First Division status. The Thames-side stadium, one of the best in the country at the time, attracted good crowds, but. First Division status would further increase attendance and there would be the prospect of West London League encounters with the well-supported Chelsea (some of whose support Norris, no doubt, hoped to purloin).

The Football League would have none of this, but Norris, as was his wont, came up with an alternative proposal, that Arsenal and Fulham could use Craven Cottage on alternative Saturdays. This of course had financial attractions for all concerned. But other London clubs objected and both the Football Association and the League followed their members (as of course they had to), so that scheme was also a non-starter.

After all the manoeuvring, Norris found himself still a director of a Second Division club with outstanding amenities but with little prospect of getting into the top flight any time soon, while neighbours Chelsea were proving to be stern competition. He also had Woolwich Arsenal on his hands, who were a Division One outfit, albeit battling in the basement of the League, in an unfavourable location that made it hard to appeal to the players and the support they needed to survive. For Norris, the logic was infuriatingly obvious. Clearly, it made every sense to combine the best and expel the negatives to create one positive situation, but he was frustrated by his competitors who understandably did not want a giant super club on their doorstep.

The Football League were also against the ambition of one man (or two, with Hall) controlling two clubs. Although there were no technical or legal obstacles to this at the time, the League had effectively obliged Norris, having failed to convince people to accept either of his two ideas, to choose to control either Arsenal or Fulham but not both. Predictably, given Arsenal's League status, he chose to put the majority of his eggs in the Manor Ground basket.

In an age when directors and chairmen sat on boards in order to promote local civic spirit and enterprise, Norris was something of an aberration. It seems he was not averse to deploying what some might see as dubious methods that might have made him powerful enemies, but apparently none that he was unable to control.

The 1910 *Who's Who* listed Norris's interests as dining clubs, wine societies and vintage-car rallies.

He was a member of the Junior Carlton Club, Mayor of Fulham, a big cheese in the local Conservative Party and a prominent freemason. His was certainly a much used name throughout London. Being a Tory of status, he would have had to assert a certain Christian philanthropy for the sake of form and for a number of years he had a close involvement with the Battersea vestry and the local orphanage. But it seems some political and business opponents recognised him as a predatory capitalist, who gained position to use it for his own ends, causing others to be pulled into a web of alliances held together by debt in kind or deed. He was even rumoured to have influence with the Archbishop of Canterbury. Norris, of course, would deny any suggestion of nepotism used by him or in his favour, but it was rumoured His Grace may have been central to Arsenal acquiring the land on which Highbury stadium would be built.

CHAPTER 16

THE ROAD TO HIGHBURY

There was a glimmer of an on-field renaissance at the end of the 1910/11 season. Finishing 10th was a top-half performance, although there was no change the following campaign.

On Boxing Day 1911, the Gunners (15th in the League) were at home to Tottenham (four points and three places behind the League leaders Newcastle United). The game, which Arsenal won 3–1, was described as a 'mud revel' by the *Sportsman*. A local newspaper reported how the ground was 'a perfect quagmire, as water lay in a pool along the touchline'.

The weather was so bad that many supporters refused to pay the shilling entrance fee, and took up a place on the infamous sewer pipe to watch the encounter (although this vantage point was not what it once was). The press reported that there had been a near riot between fans who had paid and those who hadn't. The 'free-viewers' also included opposition supporters whose transport had failed to reach the ground on time (not an uncommon occurrence at the Manor Ground).

Trying to drum up support, a number of well-known (but mostly past their best) players had been brought to the Manor Ground, the likes of Dr Leigh Richmond Roose and Alf Common, an inside-forward or centre-forward with goalscoring credentials, who, during 1905, was the first £1,000 player when he transferred from Middlesbrough to Sunderland. But as a 30-year-old Common was overweight and certainly not the player he had once been. The hope was that his name would pull the punters and initially it did. But it soon became painfully clear Alf was no replacement for Andy Ducat, the man who had been the club's biggest asset when he was sold to Aston Villa. Common's signing was obviously an attention-grabbing tactic that backfired on Arsenal. He wasn't even close to fit and posed no threat to rival defences. But, eventually, even he had to be sold as the financial situation tightened.

* * *

After a couple of years of mid-table mediocrity, in 1913, Woolwich Arsenal suffered the indignity of finishing rock bottom, four points below fellow droppers Notts County. Chelsea, who had been promoted the previous season, were five points clear of tumbling but 10 better than the Gunners' meagre 18.

Relegation had really been inevitable for some time and it finally came following the worst playing record in the club's history. George Morrell would become the first and last (so far) manager of an Arsenal team to experience the cruel drop.

Woolwich's points, goals and wins were the lowest ever recorded in the First Division and (although they were to be equalled) remained so until the end of the two points for a win system, after which, in the 1984/85 term, Stoke City had an even worse season. But during their 1912/13 campaign Arsenal scored just 11 goals on their own ground and won a single League match at home, a record that even Stoke couldn't erase from the annals of the Football League (the Gunners' other two wins were away to Sheffield United and Manchester City). On-field disaster was reflected in the club's finances: they were reported to have just £19 in the bank at the end of this ruinous campaign, income from gates having averaged just

£200. At this time, George Allison (who would later manage Arsenal) was still working as a journalist covering Arsenal's matches, but by now he was also the club's programme editor, and he would often stand outside the ground encouraging people to enter. He would then dash into the ground and shake the hands of folk he had convinced to pay admission. Often that was the best part of the day for those persuaded in.

While Arsenal sank in the mire, throughout the country, regardless of the looming prospect of war, or more likely in response to this threat, a rebellious, cheery atmosphere pervaded public life. The music halls were full and achieving football clubs were pulling large crowds. There was not much of that feeling circulating around the Manor Ground; they had indeed lost their war in 1913.

Norris and Hall had seen this coming and had been frantically looking for a way of turning things round since the end of 1912. For Norris, the solution was dramatic if simple: move. He was convinced that to guarantee the club's survival they had to relocate nearer to the centre of the capital. In 1913, accessibility was a crucial requirement in terms of facilitating big crowds; a club needed to be located in a residential area with a large population living within walking distance of an attractive, modern ground, but the stadium would also need to be accessible to travelling supporters and thus well serviced by public transport. This had always been an obstacle to the Gunners, with even newspaper journalists disinclined to make the journey to Plumstead. George Allison's Fleet Street peers avoided making the trip from the City to the Manor Ground, and it wasn't unusual for Allison to be on his own in the roomy press box in the Tress Stand. However, he took advantage of the situation by syndicating his reports to his colleagues for publication in other newspapers.

For some time, employment in the Plumstead area had been in decline; the government had been reducing the workforce at the munitions factory to less than half the level it had been a few years earlier. People were leaving the district to seek work elsewhere or did not have money to spend on football matches. This situation meant that crowds at the Manor Ground fell to numbers comparable to the time before the club had moved to the Invicta Ground.

Norris insisted that, if the right move was made, crowds would automatically increase, which would mean that investments could be made in the team and the whole financial situation would improve. The only way in those days to get the money to buy players was to pull in the punters. For Norris, this was uncomplicated reasoning. His motive was to take advantage of and develop the market for football in Greater London, so that is where the club needed to be situated. This would also offer some hope of holding on to at least part of the support Arsenal already commanded. Ideally, the site of the new ground needed to be in a densely populated district, away from the Thames that in those days restricted access (Woolwich Arsenal had the river to the North; Fulham had it for a neighbour to the Southwest). Developing a new site would give the opportunity of staking out a new territory for football and, as far as possible, a captive audience by building it a good distance from any other big club.

Hall and Norris started negotiations for several sites including locations in Battersea and Haringey, but none came particularly close to ticking all the boxes. It seemed there would have to be at least some compromise as the options seemed confined to North or West London, with the choice of at least being in the vicinity of Spurs or Chelsea, both First Division clubs.

The land Hall and Norris found in Highbury was a

comparatively underdeveloped area. Aubert Park took up a large part of the area of interest, much of which was marked up by a couple of football fields, two cricket pitches and assorted tennis courts used by the students of St John's Hall, originally called Highbury College of Divinity, which was built in 1825 (St John's College is now located in Nottingham). These facilities were accessed via St John's Hall or through two huge wooden gates on Avenell Road.

Hall and Norris had been immediately attracted by the site's close proximity to Gillespie Road Underground Station (it was just yards from where Highbury Stadium would stand and in 1933 would be renamed Arsenal Station). This had been opened just before Christmas 1906, along with the rest of the Piccadilly Line, which ran from Finsbury Park to Barons Court. Finsbury Park was also just a short walk away but the then Metropolitan Line Drayton Park Station was closer still. Hall and Norris would have premised their search on good access to the relatively new Underground network; they knew it would not only give good access from outside the area but would also draw in new housing developments to the district and thus swell the population, and, of course, the market for football.

There were many unsubstantiated rumours about how Hall and Norris became aware of and acquired the land, involving some high-ranking Church officials and alleged dubious undertakings; there was even mention of the Archbishop of Canterbury. Given some of the sharp practices Norris was reputedly capable of, we can only speculate on how accurate those rumours were. Nevertheless, following protracted negotiations that dragged out for months, with Norris applying considerable pressure (via his rumoured 'broad range of influence') on the very powerful Ecclesiastical Commissioners, a 21-year lease was agreed on a section of this land (some six acres). St John's Hall would receive just over £20,000 (a massive sum at that time when a labourer might command the equivalent of £1.25 for a week's work – but this would help soften the blow for the otherwise other-worldly Commissioners). It was also agreed that 'intoxicating liquor' would not be served in the ground and that games would not be played on Good Friday or Christmas Day, holiday periods that many clubs had traditionally taken advantage of. The college would continue to stand at the southern end of the ground (until it was destroyed by fire in 1946, and a housing development was built on the site) and it was thought undesirable to expose students to such licentiousness.

However, within the year, Norris had dismissed most of these restrictions, and all the promised constraints eventually became defunct in 1925 when Arsenal paid out a further £64,000 to buy the whole estate outright (about 10 acres at a cost of £47,000 and £17,000 for some additional land).

The deed of transfer was signed by the Archbishop of Canterbury, Randall Thomas Davidson (as well as members of the Bench of Bishops).

During February 1913, Norris openly declared that Woolwich Arsenal would be abandoning the Manor Ground (which was eventually taken over by the War Office) and that Highbury would become the club's home ground, before the LMC had approved the move. This demonstrated his confidence but probably also says more about the strength and influence of his networking, relative to the power of any authority to prevent him from imposing his will on football.

Before the deal could be finalised, the club's shareholders had to be brought onside. In March 1913, a meeting was called at the Connaught Rooms, in Great Queen Anne Street, central London. Norris made his case in theatrical style, telling how if

Arsenal failed to move to an area that might assure bigger attendances the club would certainly perish. He told of the Highbury site and declared that it was impossible for the club to pay their way in Plumstead as there were now other League clubs in London. Norris portrayed Highbury as the apex of an equilateral triangle, with a line drawn from the Clapton Orient and Spurs grounds as the base. He reminded his audience that Woolwich Arsenal had been a member of the Football League longer than other clubs in the capital, but had lost support due to the poor location of the Manor Ground.

The next morning, the *Daily Mirror* argued, 'It would be a thousand pities if a club like The Arsenal had to put up its shutters for lack of support, seeing that for twelve years they were the only members in town of the Football League, and most people will wish The Arsenal good luck in their plucky endeavour to keep the flag flying under the most disastrous conditions in years.'

Naturally, Norris eschewed the negatives and accentuated the positives of the club moving to a location with a population of approximately 500,000, calling on potential support in Finsbury, Hackney, Islington and Holborn.

After proposing the move, it was alleged that Norris received death threats, and in recent years there has been speculation that he caddishly deliberately underinvested in Woolwich Arsenal, knowing that the subsequent poor results would lead to smaller crowds, thus making the case for relocation more powerful. But there is unlikely to be much weight to this accusation, as one of the most important reasons that Norris took even a passing interest in Woolwich Arsenal was because of their First Division status. When this was lost, it would have been a massive blow to what the Fulham magnate was trying to achieve.

It has also been suggested that Highbury had always been Norris's intended destination and that other machinations were a mere smokescreen for his true aims. Although there is no clear evidence for this, it does feel like something Norris would have been capable of, and he could have predicted this particular tactic would not be well received down in Plumstead. Letters to the local newspapers accused him of being a heartless capitalist and of flogging off the soul of the Gunners. One particular missive from a Mr Paul Donaldson, published in the *Kentish Gazette*, declared, 'Mr. Norris has decided that financial gain is more important than protecting our local club. He is making a mistake. You cannot "franchise" a football club – Woolwich Arsenal must stay near Woolwich. Would Norris advocate moving Liverpool to Manchester? People like him have no place in Association football.'

Another letter in the *Kentish Independent*, this time from a Mr Walter Bailey, was even more strident: 'There is, and has been, sufficient support to run the team on a business basis ... Many clubs in different parts of the country would be glad of such support. Woolwich has been found guilty of apathy ... because it cannot furnish the huge gates that Tottenham and Chelsea get. The most distant part of London to which they intend moving will effectively prevent those who helped to make the club, and can morally claim it as their birthright, from having anything further to do with it. Is this right?'

The North Kent newspapers featured a series of cartoons; in the *Woolwich Gazette*, it was claimed Norris was kidnapping Kent's 'only son'. But the Arsenal chairman hit back by declaring that he saw Woolwich not as part of Kent but as a district of London, and that the time had come for the club to take advantage of this.

There were more protests about Woolwich Arsenal moving to Highbury, this time from Tottenham and Clapton Orient. The Os were playing at Homerton at the time so both clubs were within four miles of Highbury but Arsenal would be closer to the centre of the city and, with that crucial Underground station, far easier to reach. Quite astonishingly, Chelsea also petitioned the LMC, perhaps remembering how Norris refused the invitation of their chairman, Gus Mears, to become a tenant at Stamford Bridge in 1905. This resulted in Mears deciding to found his own club: Chelsea FC.

Spurs, probably bitterly regretting the decision to sell their shares in Arsenal, paid for an advertisement in local newspapers in an effort to hold on to their fans. The *Tottenham Herald* contained a piece begging people 'not to go and support Norris's Woolwich interlopers. They have no right to be here.'

Tottenham and Orient also issued a joint statement that argued if 'The Arsenal' moved to the Islington area 'No club will be safe'. This seems a tad dramatic but Spurs had only joined the League five years earlier and had recently spent huge amounts of money (close to £50,000, approximately equivalent to £10m today) on ground improvements. The old main stand at White Hart Lane (demolished in 1981) had been completed a mere three years before.

It seems the people of Tottenham were equally outraged if the voice of the *Tottenham Herald* can be taken as an indication of their feelings. The *Herald* featured a cartoon that portrayed the Arsenal chairman as an incarnation of the Hound of the Baskervilles, stalking farms, in a massive spiked collar, looking to kill and devour the Spurs cockerel and its food.

Henry Waller, a journalist with the *Islington Gazette*, wrote in February 1913, 'It will be a sad day for the district if these interlopers set up stall around here. A respectable, decent neighbourhood will be transformed into a rabble-infested den of noise, and, I fear, drinking. I believe it is time that the people of Highbury rose up and gave notice of their intentions to fight this proposed move. I have no objections to Woolwich Arsenal playing in their rightful home, Kent, but simply speaking, they do not belong here.'

The Highbury natives were also restless. A football ground as a neighbour was a different prospect to a college of divinity; indeed, many even viewed it as swapping a gentle culture for a form of anti-culture, and of course it would mean a drop in house prices and rental values. The area had been a quiet location and residents did not look forward to playing host to 'undesirable elements of professional football' and a 'vulgar project'.

Islington Borough Council threw its civic weight behind the opposition and raised a petition, claiming that football clubs were intent on exploiting players in order to improve share values (which was and is of course true). They also confirmed that property prices in the district would drop. Council minutes recorded the comments of Mr Coventon of Highbury Park: 'I ask whether it is open to the Borough Council to protect the district from what, in my opinion, will be its utter ruin.'

Avenell Road resident Mr A Bailey wrote, 'There will be considerable annoyance and inconvenience suffered by the residents in Avenell Road as a result of the erection of lofty stands by the Woolwich Arsenal Football Club. Can the council please help us on this matter?'

Norris countered by claiming that the folk of Highbury would hardly know a football club existed and that tens of thousands of football supporters milling round in the area once a fortnight would boost local businesses. This won over at least the businessmen in the opposition, many of whom would, of course, gain much from just the initial construction of the stadium. Norris also exerted his considerable influence on the North London media, who, as time went on, became increasingly mute on the subject of the proposed move; the vocal meetings challenging Norris's intentions and the protest groups they were part of went unreported. In this way the voice of dissent was stifled, ensuring Norris could achieve his goals.

The LMC called a special meeting during March 1913, which stretched on after 2am in the morning, coloured by passionate argument, fervent emotion and a deal of expressed abhorrence. It seemed Norris was calling in whole sets of favours and issuing sharp 'warnings' that sent League officials running scared. William Hall was also on the committee, and the then LMC president, John McKenna, was a friend of Norris. An FA inquiry was set up to investigate the whole affair.

Hall represented Arsenal. The Putney-based metal merchant, who had served on the boards of Fulham and Arsenal, at the beginning of 1913 was elected to the LMC and as such was in a good position to do some influential political backup work to the front-man role Norris was playing. CD Roberts spoke for Tottenham and G Arbor for Clapton Orient. The ruling by the LMC was that, having never objected to other clubs moving before, they could hardly do so at that point (although they had not allowed Woolwich Arsenal to move to Fulham). Tottenham were a First Division club and Orient would be competing against Arsenal in the Second Division during that first Highbury season. Tottenham had, of course, previously objected to Clapton's election to the Southern League and then the Football League.

The resolution was adopted: 'In view of the fact that a considerable number of clubs in the League have changed their ground without application to, or consent from, the League, this Committee is unanimously of the opinion that they have no right to interfere with the proposal of Woolwich Arsenal to remove its ground to Gillespie Road. The Committee are of the opinion that there is ample population and opportunity for three League clubs within the area from which the crowds for the three clubs will be drawn; and for those reasons they decline to convene a special meeting of the League, and are of the opinion that under the rules and practice of the League there is no right to interfere.'

The statement was clearly not a ringing endorsement of the move, and there may be evidence to indicate that a minority of members were against it, but the conclusion is in the true spirit of Edwardian entrepreneurialism and the buffalo stance of shared financial class interest.

It seems curious, given that the Football League had not allowed Arsenal to move to Craven Cottage, that it was relatively unperturbed about the relocation to Highbury. Maybe the League believed that three clubs (Woolwich Arsenal, Fulham and Chelsea) being so close to one another geographically would have been detrimental. But Fulham was already close to Chelsea and with the Arsenal move to Highbury they would be in relatively close proximity to Tottenham Hotspur and Clapton Orient! It seems probable that Norris required some time to 'lobby' for support. It was not unprecedented for clubs to move, for instance Notts County had recently crossed the Trent to Meadow Lane, but such relocations had never before been challenged, probably because distances moved had been relatively short and to the benefit of other clubs and local commerce. However, no club had ever *requested* a move and the League had never asserted that they had the power to stop relocations (the refusal to countenance Arsenal's move to Craven Cottage notwithstanding).

This said, Norris argued the case for moving well, citing the fact that Birmingham and Sheffield (cities with populations of 400,000 and 250,000, respectively, at that time) were nowhere near as big as the growing metropolis of London (at that time home to over seven million people) and each of these cities was supporting two leading clubs, suggesting that North London was well able to support another team, while the city as a whole could easily accommodate four.

In the last analysis, it was taken that it was not the ground but the club that was the member. However, Arsenal's situation was unique. As the crow flies, it is just 10 miles from Woolwich to Highbury, but the time it took (and at times still takes) to travel around London made it quite a different prospect from Doncaster or Middlesbrough shifting shop a couple of miles in any direction. In the past, no club had moved to encroach on what a rival might see as their territory. South Shields did relocate to Gateshead in 1930, but by then the Football League had acted, having learned from the uproar caused by Arsenal's move, to stop members transferring to other areas without their sanction.

The final top-class match played at the Manor Ground took place on Saturday, 26 April 1913, when Woolwich Arsenal met Middlesbrough. The 1–1 draw was a relatively good result as in the previous 12 months the Gunners had won just two first-team games in Plumstead. Steve Stonley scored the last Arsenal home goal in South London.

A Kent supporter, who had decided he would not make the one-hour-plus journey to Highbury, told the *Kentish Independent*, 'Henry Norris has gambled away the club's soul. He is a Mammon worshipper. We've not heard the last of this bounder, you may be sure of that.'

He was to be more right than maybe he knew.

Arsenal would retain 'Woolwich' in their title until the following April and, although the definite article was never officially adopted, the team were transformed into 'The Arsenal'. The shortened name was made official about 12 years later when Herbert Chapman insisted on using the single word 'Arsenal' when referring to the team. Strangely, the official *Football League Fiftieth Anniversary*

History tells how: 'Thus the new Arsenal club was reborn and, on 3rd April of the following year (1914) it was given permission to drop the Woolwich from the name and was henceforth known as "The Arsenal"'. This suggested that the club had requested the change of title when, in fact, no one's permission had been sought.

For all the resistance, it is likely that the majority of people around the Highbury area were interested and excited about the new football club. The subject certainly dominated the imagination, thinking and conversation of the district. Woolwich Arsenal was a 'name' in football and was recognised as a club of some stature and potential.

The 'for and against' arguments were vociferous and there were plenty who wanted to defy the likes of the 'church fanatics' and the more well-to-do residents who had the most to lose. Fears about drinking and blasphemy in what was at the time the relative backwater of Highbury was seen by others to be countered by the excitement and life Arsenal would bring with them. This was a time before television or radio could be accessed, and even pubs were a rationed delight and generally the province of men of a certain age wherein music had to be 'licensed'.

The *Daily Gazette* had it that Woolwich Arsenal secured 'the area south of the London College of Divinity bounded by Avenell Road, Highbury Hill and Gillespie Road' on 20 February 1913. The *Athletic News* claimed this had happened in March. What is for sure is that, for all Norris's faults, admittedly after a shaky start, the Highbury era would establish Arsenal among the greatest names in world football, a much bigger phenomenon than even Norris might have imagined. But that, as they say, is another story.

CONCLUSION

THE LEGACY OF NORRIS

Henry Norris remained a well-known, if not notorious, figure in London football. When the professional game recommenced after the First World War in 1919, he was still a ruthless man, although he had just been knighted for his work in recruitment during the War, having assembled three artillery brigades from the Fulham area that played an important part in the Battle of the Somme. Norris was given the title of Colonel in recognition. He had also recently been elected as the Conservative MP for Fulham East, on the promise of 'common decency', 'family values' and 'moral strength'.

From this background, after the Great War, despite the fact that Birmingham and Wolves had finished third and fourth, respectively, in the 1914/15 Second Division season (compared to Arsenal's fifth) and that it was widely believed that Division One's relegated clubs, Chelsea and Spurs, would obtain a reprieve, Norris negotiated Arsenal a place in the First Division, seemingly regardless of the fact that Tottenham had a much stronger case for inclusion among the elite; it was perhaps the most impudent and profitable act in his audacious career in the football industry. Little can be taken from the one-time Arsenal manager Leslie Knighton's assertion that Norris corresponded with 'a few financiers here and there', in order to guarantee the vote went his way, but the fact is that Arsenal were promoted by 18 votes and Spurs managed just eight.

The Football League had decided to expand each of its divisions by an extra two clubs to a total of 22. Norris knew that, for Arsenal to get over their financial difficulties, the club had to play in the top echelon of the game. At that time the canvassing of Sir Henry Norris MP knew no bounds. He emphasised his club's length of service (although Wolves had actually been League members for longer) and loyalty to the League. He had covertly solicited all the committee members (except the Tottenham directors), insisting that Arsenal were entitled to a place in the top flight due to their huge potential support, an attractive asset at a time when income from admission was divided between the pair of clubs in competition on any given match day. He also stressed Highbury's proximity to the City, which promised visiting directors many 'advantages' compared to the fleshpots of Wolverhampton and Birmingham. Norris assured Chelsea's chairman that his club would get a place (which they did) so all but Spurs were in the bag and they were never going to agree no matter what.

For all his many idiosyncrasies, Henry Norris prevented Arsenal going the way of Darwen and Burton Swifts. Although the side had done well playing their way into the First Division as a South London club, before Norris's involvement, aside from some purple patches, their record for the most part was little better than mediocre. In the FA Cup, the club got beyond the second round (the equivalent of the contemporary fourth round) just twice between 1893 and the First World War. Although those years, 1906 and 1907, when they got to the semi-final, were the highlight of Woolwich Arsenal's pre-Highbury years, it was probably the final effects of Harry Bradshaw's influence.

Before Norris, for all their best efforts, Woolwich were sliding towards oblivion, and it was Sir Henry who would create the situation that would turn Arsenal into giants, when, in 1925, after the acrimonious sacking of manager Leslie Knighton, he secured the services of Huddersfield Town's Herbert Chapman. After Norris left Highbury, in the 1930s Chapman made his former chairman's dreams reality by transforming the Gunners into a dominant side in English football. However, oddly, Norris was to cite the dismissal of Knighton as the one decision he regretted.

The circumstances of Norris's departure from Highbury were unfortunate to say the least, although one might say things just caught up with him. In 1927, the *Daily Mail* alleged that in 1925 he had been involved in passing bungs in order to secure the services of Charlie Buchan, who was a Sunderland player at the time. This during the era of the maximum wage, and any other 'financial incentives' to tempt players to join clubs were strictly outside the Football League's regulations, but many clubs and players bent and broke the rules covertly (although it was an open secret).

The notoriously 'prudent' George Morrell had effectively lost local boy Charlie in 1910, when he declined to refund the youngster's tram fares, equivalent of about 55p. It later cost Arsenal around £2,000 to bring him back to the club.

An investigation by the FA declared that Norris had also used Arsenal's expense accounts for his personal expenses, and kept £125 from the sale of the team bus for himself. Norris sued the *Daily Mail* and the FA for libel; however, during February 1929, the Lord Chief Justice, 1st Viscount Hewart, found in favour of the FA. Norris was punished with a life ban from football. This practically broke him both physically and mentally. He more or less vanished from public life and died aged 69 on 30 July 1934.

THE FOUNDERS

David Danskin was to witness all the Gunners' successes of the 1930s. In 1936, from his hospital bed (where he was spending frequent spells by this time), he wrote to congratulate manager George Allison after listening to Arsenal's Cup Final victory on the radio, something he and his fellow founders could never have envisaged precisely half a century earlier. Later, Davie's employers honoured him with a special celebration dinner. At the age of 85, on 4 August 1948, Davie passed away in Warwick.

Jack Humble (whose belligerence towards the football authorities belied his surname) had originally opposed the idea of Woolwich Arsenal becoming a limited company and for some years he continued to have reservations about his club's decision to succumb to the mores of capitalism. However, he was to admit that, without the share issue, he was unable to see how the Manor Ground could have been maintained in a fit state year on year. So long, long before David Dein pushed forward with the Highbury Bond Scheme, Jack Humble understood that football could never fully be the working man's game.

Humble would have a 40-year connection with Arsenal and was the last original founding member to have a formal tie to the club. For most of his time with the Gunners, Humble continued to work at the Royal Arsenal as a gun inspector. During World War I, he was seconded to Sheffield and then Norway.

Jack continued to act as a director of the club until his name was implicated in the financial scandal that surrounded Henry Norris. He was obliged to resign, although he was not guilty of any wrongdoing; the Football Association deemed that, as a director, Humble should have scrutinised the chairman's handling of the club finances more closely, and suspended him from football.

Humble, one of that small group of working men of 1886 who laid the foundations of Arsenal Football Club, was to witness the FA Cup win of 1930. It must have been truly astounding for him to see the fruits of his vision. He died a few months later, in December 1931, aged 69.

In April 1948, Arsenal invited the only three living members of their first professional team of 1891 to the final game of the season against Chelsea. John Julian, Gavin Crawford and John McBean watched as the Blues were beaten 2–0 with goals from Don Roper and Doug Lishman. This was an acknowledgement of the start of things, the seeds of greatness from which all that we know and recognise as Arsenal Football Club came from – the First Gunners.

The yarn of where, how and why Arsenal started is the story of the great game, the place it sprang from and people that started it. But it also reflects the history of British society and what we have become. Football was once no more than the people who played it. Now, although these individuals are the icons of the sport, it has been recreated by the mass participation of commercialism; in the contemporary era football belongs to everyone and to no one at the same time. Who could have envisaged this in 1886? Certainly not those men who strode out to play Eastern Wanderers on that sewer-surrounded patch of dark land on the Isle of Dogs. But all things grow from small beginnings and none of us knows what our actions might create and give rise to.

Today's Gunners supporters hold a distinctive and noble heritage, but it started with the kick of a ball and the most important goal Arsenal ever scored. Fittingly, no one knows whose boot or head was responsible for putting Dial Square 1–0 up a fortnight before Christmas Day 1886. As such, something of the game remains always in the nature and character of the common man.

BIBLIOGRAPHY

I have made reference to a number of texts to illuminate statistics, facts, individual player details and match reports. I have also called on national newspapers, club and supporters' handbooks, soccer annuals, programmes featuring the club, various football magazines, club histories and Who's Who publications relating to other clubs. Autobiographies and biographies of other players and managers have informed the work as have football reference books used to confirm details.

As in most historic research, one comes across contradictory information. In some cases, I have been obliged to make judgements about what is most probable, given the contextual information.

Belton, B. (2003) *Founded on Iron* Tempus

Belton, B. (2006) *War Hammers* Tempus

Belton, B. (2008) *Birth of the Blues* Pennant Books

Butler, B. (1987) *The Football League 1888–1988. The Official Illustrated History* Queen Anne Press

Cook, C. & Stevenson, J. (1988) *Modern British History* Longman

Fabian, A.H. & Green, G. (eds.) (1961) *Associated Football* Caxton

Farror, M. & Lamming, D. (1972) *A Century of English International Football 1872–1972* Robert Hale

Finn, R.L. (1972) *The Official History of Tottenham Hotspur FC 1882–1972* Robert Hale

Fox, N. (2006) *Farewell to Highbury. The Arsenal Story* Bluecoat Press

George, C. (2005) *My Story* Century

Gibson, A. & Pickford, W. (1905) *Association Football and the Men Who Have Made It* Caxton

Goldsworthy, M. (1969) *The Encyclopaedia of Association Football* Robert Hale

Green, G. (1953) *The History of the Football Association* The Naldrett Press

Harding, J. (1991) *For the Good of the Game: The Official History of the Professional Footballers' Association* Robson

Harris, J. (1995) *Arsenal Who's Who* Independent UK Sports Publications

Harrison, P. (1989) *Southern League Football: The First Fifty Years* Harrison

Hutchenson, J. (1982) *The Football Industry* R. Drew

Hayes, D. (2007) *Arsenal: The Football Facts* John Blake

Inglis, S. (1996) *Football Grounds of Britain* Collins Willow

Inglis, S. (1988) *League Football and the Men who Made It* HarperCollinsWillow

Johnston, F. (ed) (1934) *The Football Encyclopedia* Associated Sporting Press

Joyce, N. (2004) *Football League Players' Records 1888 to 1939* SoccerData

Kerrigan, C. (2004) *A History of the English Schools' Football Association 1904–2004* ESFA

Kerrigan, C. (1997) *Gatling Gun George Hilsdon* Football Lives

Knighton, L. (1950) *Behind the Scenes in Big Football* Stanley Paul

Lindsay, R. (1991) *Millwall: A Complete Record 1885–1991* Breedon Books

Lovesey, P. (1970) *The Official Centenary History of the Amateur Athletic Association* Guinness Superlatives

Mallory, J. (1997) *Football League Tables* Collins

Mason, T. (1980) *Association Football and English Society 1863–1915* Harvester Press

Mearns, A. (1883) *The Bitter Cry of Outcast London: An Inquiry into the Condition of the Abject Poor* Leicester University Press

Midment, J. (2005) *Arsenal 100 Greatest Games* Hamlyn

Matthew, T. (2007) *Who's Who of Arsenal* Mainstream

Mears, B. & Macleay, I. (2005) *Chelsea. The 100-Year History* Mainstream

Oliver, G. (1995) *World Soccer (2nd Ed)* Guinness

Ollier, F. (1988) *Arsenal: A Complete Record* Breedon

Pickard, A. & W. (1905–06) *Association Football and the Men Who Made It* (4 vols) Caxton

Prole, D. (1964) *Football in London* Robert Hale

Roper, A. (2003) *In The Days Of Gog – The Real Arsenal Story* Wherry Publishing

Shaoul, M. & Williamson, T. (2004) *Forever England – A History of the National Side* Tempus

Smith, B. *The Virgin Arsenal Fact File* Virgin

Soar, P. & Tyler, M. (2004) *The Official Illustrated History of Arsenal* Hamlyn

Spurling, J. (2004) *Rebels for the Cause* Mainstream Publishing

Spurling, J. (2006) *Highbury. The Story of Arsenal in N5* Orion

Stenton, M. & Lees, S. (1978, 1979) *Who's Who of British Members of Parliament* Harvester

Turner, D. & White, A. (1987) *Fulham: A Complete Record 1879–1987* Breedon Books

Turner, D. & White, A. (1998) *Fulham Facts and Figures 1879–1998* Northdown

Wall, B. (1969) *Arsenal From the Heart* Souvenir Press

Wall, F. (1935) *Fifty Years of Football* Cassel & Co.

Walvin, J. (1975) *The People's Game. A Social History of British Football* A. Lane

Wigglesworth, N. (1996) *The Evolution of English Sport* Frank Cass

JOURNALS/NEWSPAPERS

Athletic News

Chatham, Rochester and Gillingham News

Daily Express

Daily Journal

Daily Mail

Daily Mirror

Daily News and Leader

Derby Post

Evening Post

Football Chat

Football News

Football Players' Magazine

Football Sun

Fulham Observer

Islington Gazette

Islington Daily Gazette

Islington Daily Gazette & North London Tribune

Kentish Gazette

Kentish Independent

Kentish Mercury

Liverpool Tribune

Motherwell Times

Newcastle Echo

Saturday Night and Football Sun

Soccer History

Sporting Chronicle

Sunday Pictorial

Sports Times

The Field

The Footballer

The Times

The Sportsman

The Weekly Herald

Tottenham Herald
Woolwich Gazette
West London Press

OTHER PUBLICATIONS
Arsenal matchday programmes up to 2008
Arsenal F.C. handbooks and yearbooks up to 2008
FA Book for Boys Match
Shoot!
Topical Times annuals
Association of Football Statisticians (AFS) Bulletin
  (various)

WEBSITE
http://www.burntisland.net/danskin.htm

ARCHIVES ETC.
1837online.com
British Library
British Library Newspapers
British Pathe
Greenwich Heritage Centre
Greenwich Libraries
Guildhall Library
Islington Libraries (Local History Centre)

BRIAN BELTON

London Metropolitan Archives
National Football Museum, Preston
The Royal Artillery Museum – Firepower
University of Leicester